In-depth Small Group Bible Studies

STUDY GUIDE

1, 2, 3 JOHN

living in the light of love

Case Van Kempen

Grand Rapids, Michigan

Unless otherwise noted, Scripture quotations in this publication are from the HOLY BIBLE, NEW INTERNATIONAL VERSION, © 1973, 1978, 1984, International Bible Society. Used by permission of Zondervan Bible Publishers.

Cover photo: GettyOne

Faith Alive Christian Resources published by CRC Publications.
Word Alive: In-depth Small Group Bible Studies
1, 2, 3, John: Living in the Light of Love (Study Guide), © 2004 by CRC Publications, 2850 Kalamazoo Ave. SE, Grand Rapids, MI 49560. All rights reserved. With the exception of brief excerpts for review purposes, no part of this book may be reproduced in any manner whatsoever without written permission from the publisher. Printed in the United States of America on recycled paper.

We welcome your comments. Call us at 1-800-333-8300 or e-mail us at editors@faithaliveresources.org.

www.FaithAliveResources.org

ISBN 1-59255-202-1

10 9 8 7 6 5 4 3 2 1

Contents

Introduction 5

Lesson 1: Letters from the Beloved Disciple 7
Lesson 2: God Is Our Light 16
Lesson 3: Completing God's Love 25
Lesson 4: Desires and Deceivers 35
Lesson 5: This Is How We Know 44
Lesson 6: Test the Spirits, Love the Saints 54
Lesson 7: Faithful Witnesses 63
Lesson 8: Truth or Consequences 75
Lesson 9: Open Door, Open Heart 86

Evaluation 95

Introduction

If one of Jesus' twelve disciples came to visit the churches in your community, what do you think he would say? Would he generally be pleased with the faithfulness, devotion, and fellowship of the believers? Would he judge that the lifestyle of church members was consistent with the Word of God? Would he say "Amen!" to the message being proclaimed?

Or would he perhaps see that false teachings were making inroads against the gospel of Jesus Christ? Would he see people making excuses for their sins and church leaders too timid to call their members to obedience? Would the apostle see the light of the gospel shining into every corner of this world's darkness, or would he see the light flickering weakly and being extinguished in some places?

When the apostle John wrote three brief letters to churches toward the end of the first century A.D., the church of Jesus Christ was entering a critical time of transition. The apostolic age was drawing to a close. John, who was probably the last surviving apostle, was now an elderly man. When his voice—and pen—fell silent, there would no longer be anyone who could say to the church, "This is what I witnessed," or, "This is what I heard from Jesus himself." A new generation of leaders had already begun to take their places in the church, and at this time they needed a strong reminder to stand firm in the faith, to walk in God's light, and to resist anyone who taught a different gospel.

John's three brief letters, all originally addressed to different recipients, appear to have been eventually circulated together. They may well have been carried around by traveling evangelists like the ones mentioned in 3 John 5-8.

By God's grace these letters are still circulating among Jesus' churches today, and the message they convey is needed now more than ever. As violence and terror lurk in dark places, the church needs to proclaim that God is light. As deception and lies have become the order of the day, the church needs to announce that God is truth. As hatred and indifference continue to add to the world's pain, believers need to show that God is love. As a material-obsessed culture continues to seek meaning in acquiring more things, the church needs to say that God is life. Any teaching contrary to these beliefs has no place in the church.

Good gifts often come in small packages. The Word of God in these brief letters is powerful, exciting, and challenging. John says exactly what the church needs to hear today, and though his words may prick our consciences at times, we emerge from this study of God's Word stronger in faith.

"This is the message we have heard from him and declare to you: God is light; in him there is no darkness at all" (1 John 1:5). May God's light shine brightly on all who study John's testimony in these letters.

—Case Van Kempen

Case Van Kempen, author of this study, is a minister in the Reformed Church in America living in Holland, Michigan. He has served churches in Clymer, New York; Franklin Lakes, New Jersey; and Holland, Michigan. He and his wife, Leigh, have three children: Abigail, Peter, and Paul. Case is also the author of *Hard Questions People Ask About the Christian Faith* (Faith Alive, 2002) and *Daniel: Daring Faith in Dangerous Times* (Faith Alive, 2003).

Beginning with what "was from the beginning."

1

1 JOHN 1:1-4

Letters from the Beloved Disciple

In a Nutshell

As we begin our study of three letters attributed to the apostle John, we first review what we know of John's life from Scripture and from the testimony of early church historians. We also examine evidence for John's authorship of the letters and begin considering some of the challenges the church was facing near the end of the first century A.D. In addition, we take a look at John's prologue to the first letter, in which he states his reason for writing: "We write this to make our joy complete" (1 John 1:4).

---

1 John 1:1-4

¹That which was from the beginning, which we have heard, which we have seen with our eyes, which we have looked at and our hands have touched—this we proclaim concerning the Word of life. ²The life appeared; we have seen it and testify to it, and we proclaim to you the eternal life, which was with the Father and has appeared to us. ³We proclaim to you what we have seen and heard, so that you also may have fellowship with us. And our fellowship is with the Father and with his Son, Jesus Christ. ⁴We write this to make our joy complete.

Is Anyone Here *Not* Named John?

A quick look through a good encyclopedia of Christianity will reveal that John was a popular name in first-century Palestine and beyond. In Greek, the name is *Ioannes;* in Hebrew, *Yohanan,* a contraction of *Yehohanan,* meaning, "*Yahweh* is gracious."

Three men who went by this name figure prominently in the New Testament. In order of appearance, they are John, the son of Zechariah and Elizabeth, also known as John the Baptist;

John, the son of Zebedee, brother of James, called to be a disciple of Jesus; and John Mark, a companion to the apostle Paul and probably the author of the gospel of Mark. Of these three, the one in the middle, the disciple, is routinely credited with writing five books of the New Testament: the gospel of John; 1, 2, and 3 John; and Revelation.

A Fisherman from Capernaum—and More

We first meet John and his brother James in the gospel narrative describing the calling of Jesus' first disciples. Shortly after being baptized in the Jordan River and tempted in the wilderness, Jesus moved from his hometown of Nazareth to the larger city of Capernaum, a fishing and trading center on the north shore of the Sea of Galilee. There Jesus spotted Peter and his brother Andrew casting their nets into the lake, and he said to them, "Come, follow me," which they did at once (Matt. 4:19-20). "Going on from there, he saw two other brothers, James son of Zebedee and his brother John. They were in a boat with their father Zebedee, preparing their nets. Jesus called them, and immediately they left their boat and their father and followed him" (4:21-22).

From this brief introduction, along with a little detective work in the other gospel accounts, we can glean some interesting details about John's life. John was a fisherman carrying on the family business with his brother. And the fact that James is usually mentioned before John implies that John was the younger brother. Luke 5:10 informs us that Zebedee's sons were fishing partners with Peter, meaning that the four earliest disciples were already well acquainted with each other. Mark's gospel adds that the Zebedee family's fishing enterprise employed "hired men" (Mark 1:20), so the business was prosperous enough to hire additional help. In addition, the presence of James and John's mother, Salome, at Jesus' crucifixion suggests that she too eventually became involved in the life and ministry of Jesus (see Matt. 27:56; Mark 15:40).

Matthew, Mark, and Luke all report that John was one of "the Twelve," Jesus' closest disciples (Mark 3:16; 4:10). John and his brother also became two of the three—along with Peter—who accompanied Jesus when he healed Jairus's daughter (5:37), when he was transfigured (9:2), and when he prayed in Gethsemane (14:33). (The gospel attributed to John curiously contains no record of these privileged occasions. In addition, this gospel account uses the name *John* to refer only to John the Baptist. John the disciple apparently refers to himself

LESSON 1: LETTERS FROM THE BELOVED DISCIPLE

in this gospel in only a few vague references, such as "this disciple" and "the disciple whom Jesus loved"—John 13:23-24; 18:15-16; 19:26-27; 20:2-4; 21:7, 20, 23-24.)

Mark also tells us that Jesus gave James and John the name "Boanerges," which means "Sons of Thunder" (Mark 3:17). Later in the gospel narrative we see why: James and John wanted to "call fire down from heaven" on a Samaritan village that refused to welcome Jesus (Luke 9:54); John rebuked a man who was casting out demons in Jesus' name and received a gentle admonition from Jesus in return (Mark 9:38-39); and James and John asked for the most favored positions in Jesus' new kingdom (Mark 10:35-45). (Matthew attributes this request to James and John's mother—Matt. 20:20-24.)

A Leader of the Church

John is mentioned in three episodes in Acts as a leader of the church—and always in association with Peter. John is the second apostle named (after Peter) as one of the eleven in the upper room after Jesus' ascension (Acts 1:13). A short time later John was with Peter when they met a man crippled from birth and healed him in Jesus' name—and were later arrested (Acts 3-4). John also traveled with Peter to Samaria to investigate Philip the evangelist's reports about the salvation of many Samaritans (Acts 8:14-25).

The last biblical reference to John outside of his own books is in Galatians 2:9, where Paul describes John as one of three "pillars" of the church, along with James (see Acts 15) and Peter.

John's brother James was the first apostle to be martyred, killed at the command of Herod Agrippa (Acts 12:2). (The James mentioned in Acts 15 and Gal. 2:9 was probably James the brother of Jesus—see Gal. 1:19—who also likely wrote the book of James.)

According to church tradition, John later moved from Jerusalem to Ephesus in Asia Minor (modern-day Turkey), probably around the time Rome destroyed Jerusalem in A.D. 70 in response to a Jewish revolt. Sometime during his stay in Ephesus, John was exiled to Patmos, an island in the Aegean Sea, for preaching the Word of God (Rev. 1:9). From there, some ancient sources say, John returned to Ephesus. Others say that he traveled to Rome, and still others that he returned to Palestine. The circumstances of John's death are not known.

1, 2, 3 JOHN: LIVING IN THE LIGHT OF LOVE

Looking for a Signature
Of the five books attributed to the apostle John, only Revelation carries his signature (Rev. 1:1, 4, 9; 22:8). Though the writer of Revelation does not specifically say he was the disciple John who was called by Jesus, church history and the content of the book leave little doubt that its writer is John, the son of Zebedee.

The gospel of John contains no such identification (titles of books of the Bible were usually later additions). But on the basis of internal evidence, the evidence of other gospel accounts, unity of themes and language with Revelation, and the testimony of early church historians, the church has always accepted that the fourth gospel was written by John, the son of Zebedee.

From this identification, it's only a short step to accepting John as the writer of the three unsigned letters that also bear his name. These were apparently circulated together from the earliest days of the church as three Johannine epistles.

Overwhelming evidence pointing to John's authorship of these letters is in the vocabulary used and the themes discussed in them. Both the gospel of John and the first letter of John speak about truth, light, love, and life while also sharing nearly two dozen other key words and unique phrases. The second and third letters repeat some of the same themes, identifying their author as "the elder" (*presbyter* in Greek), an accurate description of John's relationship to the entire church near the close of the first century.

Completing John's Joy
A church in transition is often a church that can benefit from returning to first things. John took his readers back to what "was from the beginning, which we have heard, which we have seen with our eyes, which we have looked at and our hands have touched—this we proclaim concerning the Word of life" (1 John 1:1). What we discover in this first letter of John is a back-to-basics approach for dealing with heresy, disobedience, indifference, persecution, idol worship, and several other problems that were plaguing Christians toward the end of the first century A.D.

The burst of enthusiasm that marked the earliest days of the church was becoming a distant memory, five or six decades in the past. The apostolic age of the church was drawing to a close. John could see that the embers of that enthusiasm needed stirring and that some fresh fuel from his own experi-

LESSON 1: LETTERS FROM THE BELOVED DISCIPLE

ences could help keep the fire going. He was one of the last persons—if not the very last—who could inspire the church by saying, "I was there."

John wanted believers to know the truth so that their unity and singleness of purpose could be renewed and restored: "We proclaim to you what we have seen and heard, so that you also may have fellowship with us. And our fellowship is with the Father and with his Son, Jesus Christ" (1:3). The problems the churches were experiencing were affecting people's fellowship with each other and with the Lord, especially in connection with a false teaching that would become known as Gnosticism (from the Greek *gnosis,* meaning "knowledge").

As we learn in later sections of this first letter of John, there were many people who believed there was a special knowledge required for salvation, and that this knowledge rendered the physical body—and what was done with it—unimportant. The apostle Paul addressed this same controversy in his letter to the Colossians, encouraging his readers this way: "Since the day we heard about you [in your strength of faith and love], we have not stopped praying for you and asking God to fill you with *the knowledge of his will through all spiritual wisdom and understanding.* And we pray this in order that you may live a life worthy of the Lord and may please him in every way" (Col. 1:9-10; see 2:20-23). John echoes this same approach, saying, in effect, *Know God; know his Son, Jesus Christ; be filled with God's Holy Spirit; and live in obedience to God's will as revealed in his Word of life—that is, Jesus Christ.*

If the churches could return to these basics, John's joy would be complete.

Additional Notes

1:1-3—The prologue to this first letter of John draws our attention to the much longer prologue in the gospel of John, which opens this way: "In the beginning was the Word, and the Word was with God, and the Word was God. He was with God in the beginning" (John 1:1-2). Similar themes and phrases such as "from the beginning," "the Word of life," "the life appeared," and "with the Father," along with John's claim to be an eyewitness, form a strong link between these two important introductions.

As is also clear in the prologue to John's gospel, the "Word of life" that "appeared" is Jesus himself, the only way to the "eternal life" John is proclaiming (see John 14:6).

Words such as "proclaim," "testify," and "testimony" are used nineteen times in John's three letters—four times in just the first three verses.

1:1-4—The reader will have to decide whom John is referring to when he uses the word "we" in these verses. Some possible choices: (1) John is using the editorial "we" to refer to his own eyewitness testimony; (2) John is referring to a small group of original eyewitnesses, of whom he is one; (3) John is referring to the church as a body, all who believe. For my part, I think John is referring to his own eyewitness testimony as well as that of those who agree with his theological point of view.

1:4—A footnote in the New International Version points out that some early Greek manuscripts say, "We write this to make *your* joy complete" rather than "*our* joy complete."

GENERAL DISCUSSION

1. What kinds of problems do you think the church was facing as the apostolic age drew to a close? Are any of these problems still evident in the church today? Explain. How can the church best address these concerns?

2. Why does John open his letter by stating that he is an eyewitness? What's significant about his reference to several senses—hearing, seeing, and touching? What often happens to testimony—referred to as "hearsay"—when it's passed along from person to person? What role does the Bible play for us when it comes to eyewitness testimony?

3. Why is John concerned about the fellowship of the church? Wouldn't it make more sense to begin his letter by expressing concern for the doctrine or the obedience of the church?

LESSON 1: LETTERS FROM THE BELOVED DISCIPLE

4. "We proclaim to you what we have seen and heard" (1:3). What are some of the ways in which proclamation takes place? Which ways do you think are the most effective?

5. In what way was John's joy incomplete? Can our joy ever be complete if there are people who do not believe in Jesus as the Savior? Explain.

SMALL GROUP SESSION IDEAS

Opening (10 minutes)
Prayer—Open a time of prayer by reading John 1:1-5. Take a few moments to discuss the different ways in which the darkness of the world tries to hide God's light. As you pray, ask for God's light to shine brightly on this time of study.

Share—Take some time to share your expectations about this study. What do you know about John's letters already? What do you hope to gain from studying them?

Focus—This opening lesson includes a lot of biographical and historical information about John and the church near the end of the first century. As necessary as it is to have a grasp of such material, it's important to remember that these letters have a message for our day as well. Keep these questions in mind as you study together: *Would John's joy be complete if he visited the church of the twenty-first century? Why or why not? What would it take to complete his joy? Our joy?*

Growing (35-40 minutes)
Read—Since John's prologue in this first letter is quite brief, you may wish to also read the prologue to John's gospel account (John 1:1-18) and John's prologue to Revelation (Rev. 1:1-3). What do these texts have in common? What do they show us about the apostle John?

Discuss—While responding to the questions in the General Discussion section, you may wish to use some of these additional questions.

- What do you see as some of the greatest problems the church is facing today? Are they internal or external? Which ones are a greater threat to the long-term survival of the church?

- Think about the role of a witness when giving testimony in a jury trial. If you were a member of the jury, what kinds of things would persuade you that the witness was telling the truth?

- How important is your fellowship with other believers? What kinds of things can make that fellowship stronger? Weaker? Should everyone in the church always be able to get along with everyone else? Explain.

- Do you ever think church is dull or boring? Where does the problem lie—with the message being proclaimed, the method of proclamation, or something else? Should the proclamation of God's Word always be entertaining?

- How complete is your joy? Is your joy increasing or decreasing as you grow older? What kinds of things have the power to influence your level of joy?

Goalsetting (5 minutes)
Make it a goal between now and your next meeting to increase someone else's joy in the Lord. Think about how you can make that person's joy more complete—and then do it! Will it be through some kind of proclamation? Fellowship? Be prepared to share your experience with the group next time.

Closing (10 minutes)
Preparing for Prayer—In Psalm 16 David describes the source of true joy. Read this psalm together, and share any prayer concerns you may have, especially with regard to things that tend to limit our joy.

Prayer—If you are comfortable praying with each other, take part in a closing prayer, lifting up concerns that have been raised. Ask specifically for God's help in increasing the world's store of joy between now and the next time you meet together.

LESSON 1: LETTERS FROM THE BELOVED DISCIPLE

Group Study Project (Optional)

In preparation for the next lesson, "God Is Our Light," take some time to look up verses that deal with light (for example, "You are the light of the world"—Matt. 5:14; or "Your word is a lamp to my feet and a light for my path"—Ps. 119:105). Choose a verse about light that you find particularly meaningful and prepare to talk about that verse at your next meeting.

We can't walk in the light if we lie in the darkness.

1 JOHN 1:5-10

2

God Is Our Light

In a Nutshell
John opens the body of his letter with the first of many contrasts: light versus darkness. (Love/hate, truth/falsehood, and life/death are some of the other contrasts he mentions later.) After examining the meaning of John's statement "God is light" (1 John 1:5), we consider three claims that John attributes to false teachers who were misleading people to live in darkness and error. In each case John responds with a double objection. Even after two thousand years the intensity of these objections is as illuminating as ever for believers who wish to walk in God's perfect light.

---

1 John 1:5-10
5This is the message we have heard from him and declare to you: God is light; in him there is no darkness at all. 6If we claim to have fellowship with him yet walk in the darkness, we lie and do not live by the truth. 7But if we walk in the light, as he is in the light, we have fellowship with one another, and the blood of Jesus, his Son, purifies us from all sin. 8If we claim to be without sin, we deceive ourselves and the truth is not in us. 9If we confess our sins, he is faithful and just and will forgive us our sins and purify us from all unrighteousness. 10If we claim we have not sinned, we make him out to be a liar and his word has no place in our lives.

Let There Be (Only One) Light
A member of a church I served seemed to have had too much time on his hands. One Saturday afternoon I saw him just outside the sanctuary concentrating all his attention on the ceiling. "What are you up to?" I asked.

"Well," he said, "this will sound crazy, but I've always wondered how many lightbulbs we have in the church."

LESSON 2: GOD IS OUR LIGHT

"You're right," I answered jokingly. "That does sound a little crazy."

The next morning at our fellowship time, the same man came up to me and asked, "So, do you want to take a guess?"

It took me a moment to remember what he was talking about. When I recalled his lightbulb counting, I said, "Hmmm . . . a couple of hundred?" I thought I was guessing on the high side.

"Not even close," he answered triumphantly. "There are over 1,400 different lights in this church!"

I never would have guessed there were so many different sources of light in that one building.

This little story helps to illustrate a spiritual problem for many members of the church. Just as we use many different lightbulbs to chase away darkness and we seldom pay much attention to them as we flip a switch, so also we draw spiritual illumination from many different sources, often without thinking carefully about the source it's coming from. In our Scripture for this lesson John teaches us to be wary of self-proclaimed, inadequate lights.

To Illuminate the Dark Is to Eliminate It

For John, any reference to darkness is an indication of sin's presence in the world, while light is always associated with God. "God is light, in him there is no darkness at all" (1 John 1:5). John is not the first person to describe God in terms of light. See, for example, Exodus 13:21, which speaks of God as a "pillar of fire to give [the people] light," guiding the Israelites through the wilderness at night. Or consider King David's confession in Psalm 27:1: "The Lord is my light and my salvation—whom shall I fear?"

John's gospel account gives us many more examples:

- "In him was life, and that life was the light of men. The light shines in the darkness, but the darkness has not understood it" (John 1:4-5).

- "This is the verdict: Light has come into the world, but men loved darkness instead of light because their deeds were evil. Everyone who does evil hates the light, and will not come into the light for fear that his deeds will be exposed. But whoever lives by the truth comes into the light, so that it may be seen plainly that what he has done has been done through God" (John 3:19-21).

- "When Jesus spoke again to the people, he said, 'I am the light of the world. Whoever follows me will never walk in darkness, but will have the light of life'" (John 8:12).

From these few passages, we begin to understand John's meaning when he declares that God is light. And this description only begins to illuminate the richness of God's character and amazing power. But it's a helpful description by way of contrast: if sin and everything associated with it is represented by darkness, then God is represented by perfect light. "In him there is no darkness at all" (1 John 1:5).

False Claim 1: Fellowship with God in Darkness
The incompatibility of light and darkness—both can't be in the same place at the same time—is the key to understanding John's objection to the first claim of the false teachers. "If we claim to have fellowship" with God, says John, and yet we "walk in the darkness, we lie and do not live by the truth" (1:6). Having fellowship with God means we are living in God's light, while walking in darkness means we are choosing the way of sin. This is an impossible combination. Note the single claim—"to have fellowship with [God]"—and the double objection—"we lie and do not live by the truth." This pattern is repeated in 1:8 and 1:10.

To understand John's objection, imagine a violinist in a symphony orchestra who is playing independently, paying no attention to the score, the other musicians, or the conductor. Next imagine that this violinist claims to be in harmony with the orchestra and its leader. A quick check of the music and a look at the conductor will reveal that the violinist is lying. Though the violinist may be deaf and blind in terms of disobedience to both the conductor and the score, the simple fact that he or she claims to be in harmony with everyone else will not make it so. Similarly, anyone who claims to have fellowship with God and God's people while ignoring God's Word and will is a liar. A quick check of God's commandments will confirm that this is so.

John more fully explains his objection when he says, "The man who says, 'I know him,' but does not do what [God] commands is a liar, and the truth is not in him" (2:4). It's apparent from John's writing that false teachers who claimed to live in fellowship with God were refusing to give up the immorality and hedonism common to non-Christians of that time: "Do not love the world or anything in the world. If anyone loves the world, the love of the Father is not in him. For everything in the world—the cravings of sinful man, the lust of his eyes and the boasting of what he has and does—does not come from the Father but from the world" (2:15-16).

This false claim of having fellowship with God while continuing to "enjoy" immorality and hedonism has proven to be a persistent problem in the church. Every generation, including our own, can identify individuals who want it both ways: fellowship with God and fellowship with the world (and let's not be blind to the fact that this may include us). John reminds his readers that it is impossible to live in both light and darkness. We have to choose one or the other.

The choice is made much easier when we realize that Jesus can't walk with those who choose darkness over light. There can be no purification from sins if we refuse to let God's light expose our sins. In other words, there can be no forgiveness for people who deliberately choose to stay in the dark.

False Claim 2: We Are Without Sin

If the false teachers' first claim was impossible, their second was preposterous. They claimed to be without sin. They either rejected the belief that humans are sinful by nature, or they accepted the notion that sin only happens in the body, not in the spirit. Since they believed the physical body has no eternal significance, they claimed to be without sin. But John responds, "If we claim to be without sin, we deceive ourselves and the truth is not in us" (1:8).

Picture again the lying violinist. Let's say the violinist claims never, ever to play a wrong note—no matter how difficult the music, how sudden the change in tempo, or how challenging the conductor. When confronted with the clear difference between what he or she is playing and what is printed on the page, the violinist responds, "Well, that's not important. What matters is that I know the music in my spirit."

John contends that knowing what is right is not the same as doing what is right. It isn't enough merely to *want* to please and obey God; we also have to *do* it. And John knows we will never achieve perfection in this regard, so he immediately follows up his objection by saying, "If we confess our sins, he is faithful and just and will forgive us our sins and purify us from all unrighteousness" (1:9).

Yet in spite of God's willingness to forgive, it's important to remember that the availability of forgiveness does not give us permission to exert little or no effort in obedience. If we approach sin with an attitude that says, "Oh well, I'll just ask

God to forgive me later," we make a mockery of Jesus' death for our sins. It's as if we're saying that our adding to Jesus' suffering doesn't matter. There's a reason John mentions the blood of Jesus in verse 7. If what we do in the body truly doesn't matter, as the false teachers claimed, then Jesus wouldn't have had to shed his blood on the cross.

On the other hand, some of the false teachers also denied the humanity of Jesus, saying that he only "seemed" to have a human body (the central teaching of Docetism; from *dokein*, "to seem"). It's impossible to overstate the significance of this false claim today—as well as John's objection to it. Many people in our culture today want to deny the reality of sin. We are encouraged to believe in our own innate goodness, while any apparent sins are attributable to genetic predisposition, environmental circumstances, or just plain bad luck. Personal accountability is hard to find.

John suggests that we keep looking for it, because only when we find it and confess our sins can we lay claim to the assurance of God's forgiveness.

False Claim 3: We Have Not Sinned

This third claim seems similar to the second, but it has an important difference. If the false teachers denied being guilty of any sin that affected their fellowship with God (first claim), and if they denied having a sinful nature (that is, that their spirits were innately good—second claim), then in this third claim they were saying their behavior simply could not be labeled as sinful.

Let's imagine our violinist one more time. This musician is blithely unaware that his or her playing is disrupting the rest of the orchestra. The violinist makes little or no effort to play the right notes, since right and wrong mean nothing personally in terms of outward performance—and the conductor is staring aghast. When the conductor confronts the performer with the problem of making many mistakes, the violinist claims to have made none. The violinist refuses to accept responsibility for making mistakes in an orchestra that's never going to be perfect—even though the conductor may claim it will be.

Gnostics believed that everything having to do with the physical world was inherently flawed, so they claimed they could not be considered guilty for any so-called sins they committed here. Similarly today we see many people taking a "Why bother?" approach to moral and ethical behavior. If sin is pervasive (it is), and if we can never achieve perfection (we

LESSON 2: GOD IS OUR LIGHT

can't), then why even try? How can we be considered guilty if the game has been rigged against us from the start?

John responds with his strongest objection yet: "If we claim we have not sinned, we make [God] out to be a liar and his word has no place in our lives" (1:10). We can be confident that later in this letter John will tell us why our behavior matters. For now, we need to know that one or the other is true: either God is a liar and we are not guilty of sin, or God's Word is true and we are guilty of sin.

We know which one John believes. "God is light; in him there is no darkness at all" (1:5). Anyone who believes differently is seriously out of tune.

Additional Notes

1:5—"God is light." John is fond of using absolute terms to describe God. See also, for example, "God is love" (1 John 4:8, 16). These statements are not meant to limit our understanding of God but rather to say that God is the perfect expression of the named attribute.

1:9—To say that God is "faithful" means that God never acts in a way contrary to his own nature; we can depend on God's faithfulness to his own revealed Word. To say that God is "just" means that God cannot tolerate disobedience; it must be punished. In faithfulness to his Word, God punished our sins through his Son, Jesus, thereby assuring us of perfect forgiveness for our sins.

GENERAL DISCUSSION

1. What does it mean when John says there is no darkness in God? Is there darkness in us? How do we know? How can we eliminate this darkness from our lives?

2. What effect does sin have on fellowship, both with God and with other believers? Why is it impossible to both walk in darkness and claim to have fellowship with God? In light of this, how could Jesus enjoy fellowship with known sinners? (See Matt. 9:9-13.)

3. What evidence can you think of to show that people are sinful by nature? Explain how sin is an issue related not only to our physical bodies but also to our spiritual well-being.

4. What are some ways in which we try to "deceive ourselves" (1:8) when it comes to sin? Why do we do this? Why are we often slow to confess our sins and receive God's forgiveness?

5. What would you say to someone who claimed to be living a sinless life? How could you convince that person of his or her sin and God's forgiveness?

SMALL GROUP SESSION IDEAS

Opening (10-15 minutes)
Prayer—Open in prayer by reading Psalm 43:3 and asking that God's light and truth may be revealed to all of you as you study Scripture together.

Share—Briefly share your experiences in increasing someone else's joy in the Lord, as suggested in Goalsetting in the previous lesson.

The optional study project at the end of lesson 1 suggested a search for Scripture verses on the subject of light. If you've done this, share why a verse you've selected is significant.

Focus—Keep this focus question in mind as you work through this lesson: *What consequences can we expect, now and in the future, if we refuse to admit that we are sinners?*

Growing (30-35 minutes)
Read—You may wish to read 1 John 1:5-10 together before moving into your discussion time.

LESSON 2: GOD IS OUR LIGHT

Discuss—As time allows, use the following questions along with the General Discussion questions to explore and apply the teachings of this lesson.

- What are some of the ways in which God's light illuminates your life? What could you do to let in more of God's light?

- Why are some sins easier to confess than others (for example, breaking a traffic law versus adultery)? Which sins are harder to confess—those that involve just ourselves and God, or those that affect our fellowship with others? Explain.

- Think of some specific ways in which sin breaks the fellowship we enjoy with God or with each other. Do we know that this will be the result when we commit the sins? If so, what motivates us to commit them?

- Many people claim they are not responsible for their sins. Consider, for example, a child raised in a violent home who grows up to commit violent acts. Can this person be held responsible for his or her actions? Explain.

Goalsetting (5 minutes)
If there's a high level of trust in your group, choose prayer partners and commit to praying daily for each other, specifically asking God to shed light on areas of darkness (unconfessed sin) that may currently be hidden. (Set a time limit on this commitment, such as a month or until you meet again.) Or, as a group, make this a prayer concern for yourselves and each other between sessions.

Closing (10 minutes)
Preparing for Prayer—Acknowledge that the subject of sin—especially sins we may be in denial about—can be a very difficult, even discouraging subject. Read Psalm 43:5, and briefly encourage one another by stating why we can have hope in God. Also mention praises and requests you'd like to bring to God in prayer.

Prayer—Begin your closing prayer with Psalm 43:3, and give thanks for all the reasons we can place our hope in God. Ask the Spirit to shine God's light in all the dark places we try to keep hidden. Remember also to include prayer items people may have mentioned.

Group Study Project (Optional)
Between now and your next study session, think of situations in the world that can benefit from the intervention of a mediator or arbitrator. Examples might include labor disputes, political conflicts, disagreements between nations, or other situations in which two parties seek a legal or formal settlement for their differences of opinion. Take note of the parties involved, the nature of their dispute, and the role of the person(s) involved affecting the decision. Begin thinking about Christ's role as the mediator between us sinners and the holy Father (1 John 2:1-2).

The only way is to obey, walking as Jesus did.

3

1 JOHN 2:1-14

Completing God's Love

In a Nutshell

John teaches that there is only one way to know if we are living in God's love: we will walk in obedience to the Father, just as Jesus did. If we say we know God but do not walk in obedience, we show we aren't being truthful and don't really know God at all. In the same way, if we hate any of our brothers and sisters in Christ but say we walk in God's light, we are not being truthful, for hatred lurks in dark places. Only believers who obey God's Word show that they are walking in the light, completing God's love.

---

1 John 2:1-14

[1] My dear children, I write this to you so that you will not sin. But if anybody does sin, we have one who speaks to the Father in our defense—Jesus Christ, the Righteous One. [2] He is the atoning sacrifice for our sins, and not only for ours but also for the sins of the whole world.

[3] We know that we have come to know him if we obey his commands. [4] The man who says, "I know him," but does not do what he commands is a liar, and the truth is not in him. [5] But if anyone obeys his word, God's love is truly made complete in him. This is how we know we are in him: [6] Whoever claims to live in him must walk as Jesus did.

[7] Dear friends, I am not writing you a new command but an old one, which you have had since the beginning. This old command is the message you have heard. [8] Yet I am writing you a new command; its truth is seen in him and you, because the darkness is passing and the true light is already shining.

[9] Anyone who claims to be in the light but hates his brother is still in the darkness. [10] Whoever loves his brother lives in the light, and there is nothing in him to make him stumble. [11] But whoever hates his brother is in the darkness and walks around in the darkness; he does not know where he is going, because the darkness has blinded him.

[12] I write to you, dear children,
    because your sins have been
        forgiven on account of his name.
[13] I write to you, fathers,
    because you have known him who
        is from the beginning.
I write to you, young men,
    because you have overcome the
        evil one.
I write to you, dear children,

because you have known the Father.
¹⁴I write to you, fathers,
   because you have known him who
     is from the beginning.
	I write to you, young men,
	   because you are strong,
	   and the word of God lives in you,
	   and you have overcome the evil one.

Keeping Our Eyes on the Goal

Late in the game, player number 36 was racing across the floor on a fast break. He'd made a clean steal in the opponent's back court and was approaching his own basket uncontested. He could have taken an easy lay-up shot, but he'd been waiting all night for a chance to wow the crowd with one of his fancy moves. Two steps out from the hoop, he went up in the air and raised the ball for a one-handed slam. Anticipating the move, the crowd was already cheering and rising to its feet.

"Bwang!" The ball suddenly shot ten feet into the air as it bounced off the rim and flew out of bounds.

What happened? At the last second, number 36 started turning his head to watch the crowd's reaction. Because he took his eyes off the basket, his shot went wild.

Finishing well, remaining obedient to God to the end of our days, is one of the hardest lessons of the Christian life. We learn our basic Bible stories; we memorize the Lord's Prayer, the Ten Commandments, the Apostles' Creed, and maybe a few psalms; we attend church more or less regularly. But then we take our eyes off the goal of our Christian walk. Instead of keeping our focus on obedience, completing God's love (1 John 2:5), we let the world distract us, and our best efforts often go astray.

John's desire for his readers was that they stay the course of their Christian commitment. Yes, Jesus' return seemed delayed, and, yes, the church was approaching a critical transition in leadership as the voices of the apostles were being stilled. But John's voice was still strong and clear, and he reminded the church about God's unchanging call to obedience: "If anyone obeys his word, God's love is truly made complete in him. This is how we know we are in him: Whoever claims to live in him must walk as Jesus did" (2:5-6).

The More Things Change . . .

We get a sense from these verses—in fact, from all three of John's letters—that his original readers knew just what John was writing about, whereas we have to do some guesswork about the particular situations under discussion. This, of course, is part of the miracle of God's inspired Word; it speaks to every generation with equal authority. Even if we don't know the precise details or circumstances that motivated John to write, we are certainly well acquainted with our own situations!

Based on historical data about the end of the first century A.D., we can see why John's appeal for obedience seems just as appropriate now as when it was first written. Turn-of-the-first-century Christians were being lured into disobedience by the same kinds of temptations that bedevil us today at the beginning of the twenty-first century: immorality, self-indulgent prosperity, resistance to accepting diversity, misguided authority. And as the author of Ecclesiastes observed a thousand years before John, "What has been will be again, what has been done will be done again; there is nothing new under the sun" (Eccles. 1:9).

But this is not a reason to despair. Even John, with his obvious concern for what was happening in the churches, began with encouraging words in the prologue of his letter (1 John 1:1-4). And here again John writes with a mixture of affection and hope: "My dear children, I write this to you so that you will not sin. But if anybody does sin, we have one who speaks to the Father in our defense—Jesus Christ, the Righteous One" (2:1).

Defending the Indefensible

We see, then, that the first challenge is for believers not to indulge in sin. John doesn't want to minimize this call to obedience in any way; in fact, he says a lot more about obedience later in this letter. But he also wants his readers to know from the outset that any failure to be obedient is not a reason to give up trying. (That was an argument posited by the false teachers: *Since we can never achieve sinlessness, why even try?*) John reminds us all that when we do commit sins, we have an advocate who will come to our defense.

Jesus' righteousness gives him the right to bring our case before the Father, and Jesus' atoning sacrifice is our one and only line of defense (2:2). Without the free gift of Jesus' cleansing blood, not even the best defense attorney in the world could come up with an argument that could clear our name of the guilt of sin. Our case would be indefensible. But Christ has only to show the Father his hands, feet, and side, demonstrating that the debt for our sins has already been paid. Our verdict is sure: *Not guilty.*

This verdict assured by Christ has tremendous significance for everything John says in the rest of this letter. John challenges us to love one another while not loving the things of the world. He calls us to be truthful, rejecting worthless lies. He demands that we give up our idols and worship only God. Again and again John calls us to seemingly impossible ideals—to be righteous, loving, discerning, overcoming.

In each case we are not expected to be perfect, because, as we already know, that's impossible. Yet we are called to be as obedient as we can be, out of grateful love for the Righteous One who paid our debt and comes to our defense.

Obedience Is the Key
Obedience is the key that unlocks our lives to the love of God. Saying that we know God is not enough; the Christian life consists of more than mere knowledge. The person who says, "I know God," but doesn't do what God commands "is a liar" (2:4). We're also at fault if we claim that we love God while continuing to despise other people. "Anyone who claims to be in the light but hates his brother is still in the darkness. Whoever loves his brother lives in the light, and there is nothing in him to make him stumble" (2:9-10). If we walk in the light of God's love and truth, "as Jesus did" (2:6), we back up our claims that we know God and live in God.

John makes it clear that obedience to God means living by all of God's commands, old as well as new (2:7-8)—from the commandments God gave to the Israelites at Sinai to the new command Jesus gave to his disciples—teaching them to "love one another" (John 13:34). And as Jesus explains in another passage, that new command is as old as all others and inseparably tied to "all the Law and the Prophets" (Matt. 22:37-40). Obedience to the full range of God's commands is necessary to complete God's love in our lives (1 John 2:5).

It's good to remember that John's teaching is not his own creation. As he said earlier, John is passing along the message he heard from Christ himself (1:1-5). At the Last Supper, Jesus said, "If anyone loves me, he will obey my teaching. My Father will love him, and we will come to him and make our home with him. He who does not love me will not obey my teaching. These words you hear are not my own; they belong to the Father who sent me" (John 14:23-24). Even Jesus was passing along what he had been given by his Father.

LESSON 3: COMPLETING GOD'S LOVE

Pass It On

John's thoughts turn next to children, young men, and fathers. And the points he makes apply equally well to young women and mothers.

The sequence of John's thoughts in 2:12-14 is significant: "I write to you, dear children, because your sins have been forgiven on account of his name" (2:12). What a different world it would be if all children could be free from fear and doubt, secure in the knowledge of all that their Savior has done on their behalf. Parents may sometimes choose to hold out the promise of rewards as a way of encouraging obedience in children, but that is not God's way with us. God has given us the gift of salvation first, freeing us to choose obedience without the worry of having to win God's love through our behavior.

"I write to you, fathers, because you have known him who is from the beginning" (2:13). Again, what a different world it would be if we could count on seasoned believers to set a good example for those who are younger and still have much to learn in the faith.

"I write to you, young men, because you have overcome the evil one" (2:13). This may have come as something of a surprise to the young men John was writing to, just as it might today. Yet what John says is exactly right. Even those who are at a vulnerable age, struggling with decisions that can affect the rest of their lives, can put one worry out of their minds. They can be assured that Jesus has already defeated the power of evil on their behalf. They are free to choose the way of God.

Turning to "dear children" again, John says they already know the Father (2:13). How? One way is through the love they experience from godly parents, grandparents, aunts, uncles, and everyone else in the family of faith. Another is through the Word of God. Still another is through God's Spirit within them. For children nurtured in the family of faith, God makes his presence known from their earliest years.

John's second comment to the fathers (2:14) is exactly the same as his first (2:13). As John's letter unfolds, we see that one of his concerns is that people who have walked in faith even for many years can be tempted to wander from God's way. We can almost hear the combination of pleading and exhortation as John repeats, "You have *known* the Father."

Finally, John speaks again to young men, explaining his earlier comment a little more completely: "I write to you, young men, because you are strong, and the word of God lives in you, and you have overcome the evil one" (2:14). As any parent of a teenager knows, young men and women can be strong—strong physically, strong in their opinions, strong in idealism. The early adult years can be a time of many struggles, but young people who have been raised in faith are the ones who are best prepared to make their way in the world, knowing that the evil one cannot harm them.

As we reflect on these words, we can see that John's message to each group here actually applies to everyone: *Your sins are forgiven; you have known the One who is from the beginning; you have overcome the evil one; you are strong, and the Word of God lives in you.*

Though it's possible to be distracted, as player number 36 was on the basketball court, God's love for us never changes. *All* our sins have already been forgiven on account of God's Son, and we are filled with the power of God to live in obedience and love.

Additional Notes

2:1—"One who speaks . . . in our defense" is a translation of the Greek word *parakleton*, which can mean "advocate, comforter, counselor." In the New Testament this word is most often used in reference to the Holy Spirit. See, for example, John 14:16, in which Jesus promises the disciples that he will ask his Father to send "another Counselor [*parakleton*]" to be with them forever.

2:2—"atoning sacrifice." We gain a fuller understanding of what John means by this term when he writes in 4:10, "This is love: not that we loved God, but that he loved us and sent his Son as an atoning sacrifice for our sins." Other Bible translations render the Greek word here (*hilasmos*) in different terms, such as "propitiation" (KJV) and "expiation" (RSV).

2:4—"I know him." With these words John seems deliberately to be reclaiming the concept of *knowledge* for believers in Christ. The false teachers of Gnosticism claimed to have special knowledge of God and salvation, but their actions were inconsistent with God's Word. (See Titus 1:16: "They claim to know God, but by their actions they deny him.") John correctly declares that true knowledge results in obedience.

2:5—Our obedience makes God's love "complete" in us in much the same way that supplying a car with gasoline completes its purpose. Until it's fueled, it may be a beautiful, well-designed machine with lots of potential, but it isn't going anywhere. Only when that critical component, fuel,

LESSON 3: COMPLETING GOD'S LOVE

is added can the car do what it was designed to do. In a sense, obedience is the fuel that helps us complete God's loving purposes in us. Of course, our obedience isn't even possible without the empowering of the Holy Spirit, but once we're powered by the Spirit, we are called to act in obedience to make God's love complete.

2:7-8—The "new command" John is referring to is most likely the one Jesus gave at the Last Supper: "A new command I give you: Love one another. As I have loved you, so you must love one another" (John 13:34).

2:8—John's reference to "the true light" reminds us of the opening words to John's gospel: "The true light, which enlightens everyone, was coming into the world" (John 1:9).

GENERAL DISCUSSION

1. Even from a brief reading of Scripture we can see that obedience is important to God (see, for example, Gen. 2:15-17). Why? What does obedience signify? What are some of the reasons John gives for living in obedience to God's commands?

2. What does it mean to "walk as Jesus did" (1 John 2:6)? Think about not only doing good and helping others but also denying oneself, suffering for the sake of others, and possibly even laying down one's life. Does God expect the same measure of Christlike obedience from every believer? Explain.

3. Who is my "brother" (1 John 2:9)? (Jesus answered a similar question in Luke 10:29-37.) Why is it important for me to love my brother, sister, neighbor? What if my brother hates me with a passion and is willing to commit unspeakable acts of cruelty against me? Am I commanded to love even such a hate-filled person?

4. How does hatred cause us to stumble?

5. In what ways do children, young adults, and older adults perceive obedience differently? How does the passing of time change our attitudes toward obedient living?

SMALL GROUP SESSION IDEAS

Opening (10-15 minutes)
Prayer—Read Psalm 119:1-8. Ask God to direct this time of study, to use it to teach the blessings of obedience, and to create in each of you a heart that desires light more than darkness.

Share—The optional group study from session 2 invited you to take note of situations in the world that might benefit from the intervention of a mediator or arbitrator. What kinds of situations did you observe since your last meeting? What role did disobedience play in creating conflicts? What kind of mediator, if any, was called in to help resolve an issue?

Focus—In a word, this lesson is about *obedience*. In our Scripture for this lesson John builds a case to encourage his readers to turn or return to the way of faithful obedience to God's commands. Keep these questions in mind during this time of study: *On a scale of 1 to 10, with 1 representing a complete scofflaw and 10 representing Christlike perfection, how would I rate my obedience to God's commands? What score would others give me? Does my score change for better or worse as I consider John's teaching?*

Growing (30-35 minutes)
Read—Before reading 1 John 2:1-14 together, scan the passage, noting how often John uses the word "sin" or a word pointing to sin, such as "liar," "hates," "darkness," and "blinded." Next observe how often John refers to obedience, using phrases such as "do what he commands," "truth," "love," "live," and so on. Then read the verses aloud.

LESSON 3: COMPLETING GOD'S LOVE

Discuss—Select and discuss General Discussion questions that best fit the needs of your group. As time allows, choose also from the following questions, which may help people in processing John's teaching personally.

- Does today's church need a strong voice to say, "I write this to you so that you will not sin"? If so, who might be that voice? Could it be that we are the ones who are supposed to call the church back to obedience? Explain.

- What feelings arise when you read that Christ has come to our defense? What are some ways in which we can show those same feelings in every part of our lives?

- List some examples of people who know the rules but choose not to obey them (think about athletes, corporate executives, drug dealers, and so on). What's the usual result when knowing does not result in doing?

- Can you think of any examples of people who claim to know God but choose to follow a path that's not in line with God's commands? What effect does their disregard for obedience have on the rest of the church?

- If you were (or are) an older adult and could pass along only one piece of advice to the next generation, what would it be?

Goalsetting (5 minutes)
Think about an important bit of advice you could pass along to someone in the next generation (as mentioned in the last question of the preceding *Discuss* section). Make it a goal between now and the next session to share that advice with someone (such as your own child or grandchild, another young relative, a college student in your church, a younger coworker). You may also wish to talk about this Bible study and share with that person your desire to live obediently—and for him or her to do the same. (In my own experience I've learned that these kinds of thoughts, conveyed with humor and sensitivity, can have a profound and lasting impact on the recipient.)

Closing (10 minutes)
Preparing for Prayer—If obedience were easy, we could probably do away with about two-thirds of the Bible. But obedience takes a lot of conscious effort, so it's definitely an appropriate subject for prayer. God wants to help us in our obedience. Think and talk about this important truth together, and con-

sider sharing other joys or concerns you might have as you prepare for prayer.

Prayer—After a few moments of silence, offer brief prayers of thanksgiving for Christ's sacrifice for our sins. Continue with one- or two-word descriptions of areas in which greater obedience is needed in your lives (for example, *work, school, television watching*; vague wording is fine). Conclude with thanksgiving for the responses God will give. Make sure also to include the prayer concerns and praises people have mentioned.

Group Study Project (Optional)
The second half of 1 John 2 deals with the world and its desires, followed by a section on deceivers (antichrists) who deny that Jesus is the Christ. To prepare for lesson 4, see if you can bring in or report on the most outrageous example of either a desire or a deceiver (for example, solid gold shoehorns, or people who claim to talk to the dead). The more extreme, the better!

Cravings, pride, lies—and our indelible anointing.

4

1 JOHN 2:15-27

Desires and Deceivers

In a Nutshell

Love of God or love of the world? Truth or lies? An anointing that is real or one that is counterfeit? Jesus Christ or antichrists? With this series of stark contrasts John challenges his readers to remain on the path leading to eternal love, eternal truth, eternal life.

---

1 John 2:15-27

¹⁵Do not love the world or anything in the world. If anyone loves the world, the love of the Father is not in him. ¹⁶For everything in the world—the cravings of sinful man, the lust of his eyes and the boasting of what he has and does—comes not from the Father but from the world. ¹⁷The world and its desires pass away, but the man who does the will of God lives forever.

¹⁸Dear children, this is the last hour; and as you have heard that the antichrist is coming, even now many antichrists have come. This is how we know it is the last hour. ¹⁹They went out from us, but they did not really belong to us. For if they had belonged to us, they would have remained with us; but their going showed that none of them belonged to us.

²⁰But you have an anointing from the Holy One, and all of you know the truth. ²¹I do not write to you because you do not know the truth, but because you do know it and because no lie comes from the truth. ²²Who is the liar? It is the man who denies that Jesus is the Christ. Such a man is the antichrist—he denies the Father and the Son. ²³No one who denies the Son has the Father; whoever acknowledges the Son has the Father also.

²⁴See that what you have heard from the beginning remains in you. If it does, you also will remain in the Son and in the Father. ²⁵And this is what he promised us—even eternal life.

²⁶I am writing these things to you about those who are trying to lead you astray. ²⁷As for you, the anointing you received from him remains in you, and you do not need anyone to teach you. But as his anointing teaches you about all things and as that anointing is real, not counterfeit—just as it has taught you, remain in him.

What a Wonderful but Temporary World

Many of us who live in northern parts of the United States and in Canada know that when winter arrives, our cars will be covered with snow, slush, and salt. As much as we appreciate the safety of driving on roads cleared of icy spots, we often cringe when we see crusty white lines of road salt creeping up the sides of our vehicles. And we know that after only a few winters we'll find rust developing right where the salt is thickest. As a result, it's not uncommon to see ads for used cars—especially sports cars, convertibles, and collectibles—boasting the phrase "never driven in snow," because many people put their prized vehicles into storage as soon as the snow season begins.

When our family lived in New Jersey, we saw that there was generally less snowfall—and less road salt—than in New York and Michigan, so it wasn't unusual to see "summer" cars on the road even in the middle of winter. People might not drive around with the top down, but neither did they worry much about the effects of road salt.

Still, even the most cautious, car-loving drivers occasionally got surprised. At a gas station in Franklin Lakes one morning, after an unexpected, heavy snowfall, there in front of me was a Ferrari Testarossa, an exotic car that costs as much as some nice homes, and its gorgeous red finish was covered with salt.

What was it Jesus said about laying up treasures on earth? Something about moths and thieves—and rust? (See Matt. 6:19-21.) No matter how much we love things of this world, no matter how carefully we try to preserve them, no matter how strong our desires are for them, they're all temporary. If we place our hopes on them to bring us joy and satisfaction, we'll be disappointed every time.

Doc, I've Got These Cravings

Even though we know all this, we can't seem to tear our eyes away from the world's temptations. John describes this affliction in three parts as "the cravings of sinful man, the lust of his eyes and the boasting of what he has and does" (1 John 2:16). A more literal translation of the Greek text here renders these as "the lust of the flesh and the lust of the eyes and the vainglory of life."

Some Bible scholars have suggested that these three vices parallel the temptations Jesus faced in the wilderness—the temptation to focus on his own physical needs, the temptation to be sensational in the eyes of the people, and the temptation to take prideful possession of the whole world apart

LESSON 4: DESIRES AND DECEIVERS

from obedience (see Matt. 4:1-11). While we can't be sure whether John was drawing parallels to Jesus' temptations here, we can note similarities and recognize that these may simply be the temptations that are most common to humanity.

To the believers John was addressing, false teachers may have been holding out the promise of physical pleasure as a part of their corrupt worship rituals (see, for example, 1 Cor. 6:12-20, where Paul appears to be talking about prostitution in the Corinthian temple to Aphrodite). We hardly need to mention how immorality is portrayed in the media today. People who engage in sex outside of marriage are often depicted as joyful, free, and part of the "in" crowd, while marriage is shunned as confining and controlling.

In addition to sexual sins, a religion of "consumerism" seems also to have taken hold in our culture, even among many who claim to be faithful followers of Jesus. Symptoms of this illness include compulsive shopping, stockpiling, extravagance (have you seen the hot tub that comes with the built-in, wide-screen home theater system?), and "keeping up with" friends and neighbors ("Well, if they go to that new theme park or ritzy golf course or buy that furniture, I guess we should too").

But giving in to our cravings does not bring greater happiness. We hardly need an expert to convince us that people with more stuff are no happier than those with fewer or less expensive possessions. Contrary to what the bumper sticker says, "the person who dies with the most toys" does not win anything!

And yet we still struggle with lusts of the flesh. We need to believe John when he says that "the world and its desires pass away" (1 John 2:17). Just ask the guy with the salty Ferrari!

What's That in Your Eye?

If the "cravings of sinful man" have to with physical and material gratification, the second item John mentions—"the lust of [the] eyes" (2:16)—refers to covetous desires, whether acted on or not.

Unless we live in a cave isolated from most aspects of "civilization," it's hard to avoid being bombarded with advertising for every conceivable consumer product. Even if I never have the cash to go out and buy a TV-equipped hot tub, simply the fact that I've seen an ad for one can create dissatisfaction and desire within me (not really, but you get the idea). At its very foundations, consumer advertising is designed to make us want something we don't have.

Sometimes we might wish we could use the same techniques to create a desire for faith—but we can't. Much of today's advertising is based on deception, exaggeration, or "bait-and-switch" techniques. Have you ever gone to a car dealer and tried to actually buy the car advertised for "no money down, and only $199 a month"? Why did it turn out to be more like $299 a month by the time the deal was done?

We can't use deceit to sell faith. We have to proclaim it on its merits, the greatest of which is that faith endures for eternity when all other objects of our desires have faded away.

Oh, Yeah? My Hot Tub Has a 50-Inch Screen!

John's third observation about the world and its desires relates to boasting. Apparently the compulsion to brag about our status or possessions is not a new phenomenon.

"The boasting of what [a person] has or does" consumes far too much of our energy, wastes precious resources that could help to enrich someone else's life, and, even worse, destroys fellowship. Instead of cooperation and unity in the church, we often find competition and disharmony.

The apostle Paul ran into this problem in Corinth also. Hearing that some were gorging themselves at the celebration of the Lord's Supper while others went hungry, Paul wrote, "Don't you have homes to eat and drink in? Or do you despise the church of God and humiliate those who have nothing?" (1 Cor. 11:22). This is what our "vainglory" (excessive pride) accomplishes: lack of respect for the church and the humiliation and alienation of its members.

Antifellowship, Antitruth, Antichrists

From worldly desires John turns to warn about worldly deceivers. "Dear children, this is the last hour; and as you have heard that the antichrist is coming, even now many antichrists have come. This is how we know it is the last hour" (1 John 2:18).

The "last hour" John is referring to is the time in which we are still living—the time between Jesus' resurrection and his return. Antichrists who had already appeared were former members of the church—at least in appearance (2:19). They spread lies about Jesus, denying that he was the Christ (2:22), and they were actively trying to get others to join them on their path of disobedience (2:26).

LESSON 4: DESIRES AND DECEIVERS

John's title for them, "antichrists," has given rise to a great deal of speculation about events that will take place before Jesus' second coming. If we allow Scripture to be our guide, however, we see that the concept of antichrists began with Jesus' teaching in which he described the last days. "Many false prophets will appear and deceive many people," Jesus said (Matt. 24:11). "So when you see standing in the holy place 'the abomination that causes desolation,' spoken of through the prophet Daniel . . . then there will be great distress, unequaled from the beginning of the world until now—and never to be equaled again" (24:15-21). Jesus concluded, "At that time if anyone says to you, 'Look, here is the Christ!' or 'There he is!' do not believe it. For false Christs and false prophets will appear and perform great signs and miracles to deceive even the elect—if that were possible" (24:23-24).

"False Christs" became known as antichrists, and a quick review of Daniel shows that there was one particularly cruel and oppressive king, Antiochus IV Epiphanes, who may have been regarded as the prototype for antichrists that would rise to prominence from time to time in the last days (see Dan. 7-8; 11-12).

Paul describes such an ultimate deceiver as "the lawless one" who displays "all kinds of counterfeit miracles, signs and wonders" (2 Thess. 2:9), and John describes impostors such as "a beast coming out of the sea" and a beast "coming out of the earth" to deceive, especially with the use of amazing power (see Rev. 13-19). What we need to remember from John's letters is that there can be more than one antichrist. In fact, it's pretty clear that every generation has been plagued by people who have "the spirit of the antichrist" (1 John 4:3).

John is convinced that these deceivers never really belonged to the church. "For if they had belonged to us, they would have remained with us; but their going showed that none of them belonged to us" (2:19). *Remain* is a key word for John. He uses it four more times in our passage for this lesson (2:24, 27) as he pleads for the faithful members of Jesus' churches to stay true to the course of their faith. (See also Jesus' teaching in John 15:1-17.)

Counterfeiters Will Be Prosecuted

Another key word for John was *anointing,* his term for the presence of God's Holy Spirit in all who belong to Christ. "You have an anointing from the Holy One, and all of you know the truth" (2:20). Much has been made of this word in recent years, so much so that some believers fear they may not be sufficiently "anointed" as believers even though they have received Christ as their Savior.

John himself shows that this concern has no basis in Scripture. He says, "All of you know the truth"—not just people who claim a special anointing. "The anointing you received from him remains in you, and you do not need anyone to teach you" (2:27). This certainly suggests that we cannot lose our anointing from the Holy Spirit and that there is no greater anointing that comes to only a few specially chosen believers. Neither is there any anointing apart from God's Holy Spirit; anyone who claims such a thing is promoting a counterfeit anointing (2:27).

Our anointing is a gift from God that allows us to believe in Jesus, and John desires that we remain true to this anointing. No worldly desire or deceiver can take our anointing away. It's a treasure that neither moths nor thieves nor rust can destroy.

Additional Notes
2:15-17—John refers to "the world" (*kosmos* in Greek) metaphorically. So he is not saying we should despise God's creation and everything in it; after all, John also records that "God so loved the world that he gave his one and only Son" to save it (John 3:16). Here John is using this term to distinguish a life lived with God from a life lived apart from God—that is, entirely concerned with this world.

2:18-19, 22—John is the only New Testament writer to actually use the word "antichrist," which simply means "against Christ." It's important to note that John sees antichrists as coming from within the church itself, rather than appearing on the scene as representatives from other religions or world powers.

2:22-23—Just as John uses the words "anointing" and "remain" to plead with and encourage believers who are faithful, he also uses the word "deny" several times to describe false teachers. One of the major heresies of John's day was the denial of Jesus' divinity: "Who is the liar? It is the man who denies that Jesus is the Christ."

LESSON 4: DESIRES AND DECEIVERS

GENERAL DISCUSSION

1. John cites three categories of worldly desires (1 John 2:16). What effects do these desires have on the fellowship of the church? Why? What are some ways in which believers can help each other resist these vices?

2. John regarded the presence of antichrists as a sign that the church was living in "the last hour" (1 John 2:18). Who are today's antichrists, and where do we find them? What are they saying about Jesus? What influence is their activity having on the church?

3. What is our "anointing from the Holy One" (1 John 2:20), and how does this help us know the truth? What does John mean when he says, "The anointing you received from him remains in you, and you do not need anyone to teach you" (2:27)?

4. Why did the false teachers deny that Jesus was the Christ (1 John 2:22)? Why couldn't they just acknowledge that he was the Christ, the Son of God, and continue in their world-loving ways?

SMALL GROUP SESSION IDEAS

Opening (10-15 minutes)

Prayer—Since a significant part of this lesson deals with false teachers, read Psalm 94:1-11 together. After a moment of quiet, share your reactions to these verses. Begin a time of prayer by asking God to bless your group with a full measure of truth during this session.

Share—If any of you followed the suggestions of the Goalsetting section of session 3, talk about what it was like to pass along advice or wisdom to someone of the next generation. How did it feel to tell someone else what you have learned?

Focus—This lesson has a double focus: desires and deceivers. The first has to do with temptations the world places in our path in line with our desires; the second deals with false teachers who try to draw us away from following Jesus. To help concentrate on both aspects of the lesson, keep these questions in mind: *When I'm faced with worldly desires and temptations, what is my weakest area of resistance? How might someone try to exploit this weakness to draw me away from the path of faith?*

Growing (30-35 minutes)
Read—You may wish to read and discuss the Scripture for this session in two parts: 1 John 2:15-17, followed by General Discussion question 1; and then 2:18-27, followed by questions 2-4. Note John's repeated use of several key words—*remain, deny, anoint*—in the second part of the passage.

Discuss—These additional questions follow the pattern of the questions in the General Discussion section. The first one relates to John's teaching about worldly desires, and the others deal with problems caused by deceivers.

- How does the love of a worldly lifestyle distract us from our calling as Christians? How effective can we be in drawing others to Jesus if it appears that our own material comfort and security are our top priorities?

- How do we know we have received an anointing from the Holy One? Will we look different? Act different? Feel different? Explain.

- "I am writing these things to you about those who are trying to lead you astray" (1 John 2:26). Why are false teachers concerned about having people follow them? Who is motivating them to act? How do we know if a person's teaching is real or counterfeit?

- Is there a new gospel message for each generation? If not, how do we convince people who are always looking for "the latest thing" that "the old, old story" is still the only way to eternal life?

Goalsetting (5 minutes)
It's hard to practice material self-denial and spiritual self-discipline when we're pressured every day to indulge in worldly pleasures and to listen to worldly teachings. When so many

seemingly well-intentioned people appear to live comfortably and try to tell us that our way of faith is quaint and old-fashioned, it can be hard to stay the course of faithfulness. It may be even harder to persuade the next generation to follow that course.

Between now and the next session, decide on one specific way you can live more simply and be less likely to be affected by worldly temptations. Make this a subject of prayer, and ask God to help you steer your life less toward the world and more toward God.

Closing (10 minutes)

Preparing for Prayer—Turn again to Psalm 94, and this time read verses 12-15. As the psalmist makes clear, we need the discipline of the Lord if we're going to remain obedient to the teaching of God's Word. Discuss personal prayer concerns as well.

Prayer—Open your prayer with a brief time of silence so that everyone can focus their thoughts on God. Pray for the strength to turn away from sinful desires and deceivers. Pray also for specific concerns that have been mentioned.

Group Service Project (Optional)

With five sessions to go in this study, this might be a good time to think about a group service project. Based on what John says in this chapter about turning away from worldly desires, consider holding or sponsoring a group auction as a fund-raiser. You could do this on a small scale together on the Internet using eBay, for example. Or you could spread the word throughout your church and surrounding community, inviting others to join in and give for a good cause.

Have some fun deciding how best to use the collected funds to teach about the joy of staying on the path of faith. Maybe you could sponsor a youth or adult work project, or perhaps you could help pay for camp scholarships or help with a seminarian's tuition. The idea is to take something of this world and turn it into something that benefits the kingdom of God—giving God the glory!

Four critical questions on the road to remaining.

5

1 JOHN 2:28-3:24

This Is How We Know

In a Nutshell
In our Scripture for this lesson, John first reminds us that we are children of God, challenging us to live in a way that's fitting for children who want to be like their Father. Then John answers four critical questions to help us in our efforts to remain faithful:
- Who are God's children?
- What is love?
- How do we know we belong to the truth?
- How do we know God lives in us?

---

1 John 2:28-29
28And now, dear children, continue in him, so that when he appears we may be confident and unashamed before him at his coming.

29If you know that he is righteous, you know that everyone who does what is right has been born of him.

1 John 3
1How great is the love the Father has lavished on us, that we should be called children of God! And that is what we are! The reason the world does not know us is that it did not know him. 2Dear friends, now we are children of God, and what we will be has not yet been made known. But we know that when he appears, we shall be like him, for we shall see him as he is. 3Everyone who has this hope in him purifies himself, just as he is pure.

4Everyone who sins breaks the law; in fact, sin is lawlessness. 5But you know that he appeared so that he might take away our sins. And in him is no sin. 6No one who lives in him keeps on sinning. No one who continues to sin has either seen him or known him.

7Dear children, do not let anyone lead you astray. He who does what is right is righteous, just as he is righteous. 8He who does what is sinful is of the devil, because the devil has been sinning from the beginning. The reason the Son of God appeared was to destroy the devil's work. 9No one who is born of God will continue to sin, because God's seed remains in him; he cannot go on sinning, because he has been born of God. 10This is how we know who the children of God are and who the children of the devil are: Anyone who does not do what is right is not a child of

God; nor is anyone who does not love his brother. [11]This is the message you heard from the beginning: We should love one another. [12]Do not be like Cain, who belonged to the evil one and murdered his brother. And why did he murder him? Because his own actions were evil and his brother's were righteous. [13]Do not be surprised, my brothers, if the world hates you. [14]We know that we have passed from death to life, because we love our brothers. Anyone who does not love remains in death. [15]Anyone who hates his brother is a murderer, and you know that no murderer has eternal life in him.

[16]This is how we know what love is: Jesus Christ laid down his life for us. And we ought to lay down our lives for our brothers. [17]If anyone has material possessions and sees his brother in need but has no pity on him, how can the love of God be in him? [18]Dear children, let us not love with words or tongue but with actions and in truth. [19]This then is how we know that we belong to the truth, and how we set our hearts at rest in his presence [20]whenever our hearts condemn us. For God is greater than our hearts, and he knows everything.

[21]Dear friends, if our hearts do not condemn us, we have confidence before God [22]and receive from him anything we ask, because we obey his commands and do what pleases him. [23]And this is his command: to believe in the name of his Son, Jesus Christ, and to love one another as he commanded us. [24]Those who obey his commands live in him, and he in them. And this is how we know that he lives in us: We know it by the Spirit he gave us.

Wha'd'ya Know?

Humorist Michael Feldman, host of a live weekly radio program on many public radio stations, always begins his show by telling a joke or a funny story. After the laughter dies down, he pauses for a moment and then says, "So wha'd'ya know?" His audiences have been trained to respond, in unison, "Not much. You?"

If the apostle John wasn't writing about such a serious subject—the survival of the church—he might appreciate this little bit of comedy business. But John wasn't joking around. He saw all too clearly that some members of the church were acting as if they didn't know much. Either they had forgotten the message they had heard since the beginning (1 John 3:11; see 2:24), or they were willing to be swayed by the latest false teaching.

In the first half of our passage for this lesson John distinguishes between children of God (3:1-2) and children of the devil (3:8). In the second half John makes a distinction between those who love (3:11, 14) and those who hate (3:12-15). In both parts—and we cannot say this strongly enough—*the difference is revealed through the deliberate, visible behavior of individual believers.* "Anyone who does not do what is right is not a child of God" (3:10). "If anyone has material possessions and sees his brother in need but has no pity on him, how can the love of God be in him?" (3:17).

In response to the question "Wha'd'ya know?" John never wants a believer to answer, "Not much." He tells us exactly what we need to know to be children of God who show that we have God's love in our lives.

Are We There Yet?
It's hard to know if the last two verses of 1 John 2 complete John's thought about remaining in the Lord ("Remain in him. . . . Continue in him"—2:27-28), or if John is starting a new section by introducing the idea that believers who do what is right while awaiting Christ's return show that they have been born of God (2:29). There's no reason these two verses can't serve both purposes, but let's concern ourselves here with the newly introduced theme of righteous living as children of God.

As any family on a car trip can tell you, the final hours of driving can seem a lot longer than the first. Similarly, that "last hour" John mentions in the previous section (2:18) has gotten to be a lot longer than expected, and the children of God in the back seat are showing signs of getting restless. John counsels patience and good behavior, promising that the wait will be worthwhile.

While we are waiting and continuing on our journey, John wants us to consider several things, beginning with our Father's love. "How great is the love the Father has lavished on us, that we should be called children of God!" (3:1). As we will see several more times in this letter, love is both a gift and a command. We are loved lavishly, and we are called to extend God's gracious love to others.

Though we already know we are God's children, the world hasn't always acknowledged this fact. John, who was constantly aware of the false teachers who wanted to lead God's children astray, said that this is because the world hasn't known God (3:1). (And remember that John uses "the world" as a shorthand term for referring to people who choose not to live for God.) But if anyone doesn't know God, it's not because God hasn't made himself known. As the apostle Paul says, "Since the creation of the world God's invisible qualities—his eternal power and divine nature—have been clearly seen, being understood from what has been made, so that men are without excuse" (Rom. 1:20).

John next says a few things about our ultimate destination—namely, that "what we will be has not yet been made known," though we do know that "we shall be like [Jesus]" (1 John 3:2). While false teachers may have been making all kinds of claims about the afterlife, John knew that Jesus had only promised to come back and take his followers to the place where he was going (John 14:3). John may also have been aware of what Paul said regarding our future life with Jesus: "Our citizenship is in heaven. And we eagerly await a Savior from there, the Lord Jesus Christ, who, by the power that enables him to bring everything under his control, will transform our lowly bodies so that they will be like his glorious body" (Phil. 3:20-21).

Living Like People with a Sure Hope
Just the hope of our eternal destination should be enough to make us want to live lives that are pure and pleasing to God, says John. The only alternative is to live as children of the devil.

Notice John's repeated use of generalities—"everyone," "no one," "anyone"—in 1 John 3:3-9. "Everyone who has this hope in [Jesus] purifies himself, just as he is pure" (3:3). "No one who lives in him keeps on sinning. No one who continues to sin has either seen him or known him" (3:6). There's no middle ground here. John knows that everyone sins, regardless of their best efforts (3:4-5), but either we trust in Christ's forgiveness and try to refrain from sinning, or we make no effort regarding our sins and live like children of the devil.

John's unique argument is that "God's seed remains" in those who are born of God; they "cannot go on sinning" because they have been born of God (3:9). The Revised Standard Version of the Bible translates the word for "seed" here (*sperma* in Greek) as "nature," and this may be a helpful way to understand what John meant. Just as an apple seed grows not into an orange tree but an apple tree, so the seed of God planted in us will inevitably grow to be what God intends—revealing its true nature in changing us to do what is right, making us righteous, like Jesus (3:7; see 2:6). As we grow, not only do we desire to be like God, doing his will to the best of our abilities, but we also can't help becoming like God. God's seed gives birth to children who resemble their Father. (See 2 Cor. 3:18.)

How Do We Know God's Children?
John next delivers the first of his four "how we know" statements in this passage. (There was one in 2:5-6 also: "This is how we know we are in him: Whoever claims to live in him must walk as Jesus did.")

This statement has to do with knowing who belongs to whom—"This is how we know who the children of God are and who the children of the devil are: Anyone who does not do what is right is not a child of God; nor is anyone who does not love his brother" (3:10). Again, John clearly understands that everyone is guilty of sin; he is not saying that we're children of the devil if we're not perfect. He is looking at intent, perhaps in much the same way that we know "the LORD looks at the heart" (1 Sam. 16:7). Indeed, "God is greater than our hearts, and he knows everything" (1 John 3:20). Is the individual showing any effort to resist sin? Are God's commands being honored? Is there any sign of growing love for brothers and sisters in Christ?

As we observed before, John isn't joking around. He wants the members of Christ's church to get serious about obedience.

How Do We Know What Love Is?
In the second half of his first "how we know" statement John connects being a child of God with loving one's "brother," or neighbor (3:10). John uses the example of Cain and Abel to tell us how we can recognize sincere love. As far as John is concerned, there's no mystery about why Cain killed his brother. Cain "belonged to the evil one. . . . His own actions were evil and his brother's were righteous" (3:12). With the perspective that comes from living a long time, John keeps this very simple: *Evil actions come from an evil heart.*

Continuing, John adds, "Do not be surprised . . . if the world hates you" (3:13). Why not? Because, of course, anyone who is of "the world" has chosen not to live for God and is not a child of God and thus has no natural inclination to love others. Further, the very lives of those who are born of God, who bear God's nature, are a condemning testimony against people who have not been born of God. Just as Abel's acceptable offering made clear that Cain's was unacceptable, so the life choices of those who seek to love one another condemn the life choices of those who do not. Again, it's a matter of intent—what's in the heart. If God's seed is present, love for others will be present also; if not, there is no real love present at all—only selfishness and thus hatred for others.

"This is how we know what love is: Jesus Christ laid down his life for us. And we ought to lay down our lives for our brothers" (3:16). This matter of laying down our lives applies in more than extreme situations; in fact, it is more often revealed in the little things we do in relation to our neighbors. "If anyone has

LESSON 5: THIS IS HOW WE KNOW

material possessions and sees his brother in need but has no pity on him, how can the love of God be in him?" (3:17). Love reveals itself in all our actions.

How Do We Know We Belong to the Truth?
Truth is another thing revealed in all our actions. "Dear children, let us not love with words or tongue but with actions and in truth. This then is how we know that we belong to the truth, and how we set our hearts at rest in his presence whenever our hearts condemn us" (3:18-20). Sometimes our hearts can be riddled with doubt, especially if we've fallen again and committed those sins we most struggle with. It's as if John is saying here, "Of course we aren't perfect, but we can at least take comfort in knowing we have tried before and are trying again to act in a way that pleases God; we really want to live by God's truth."

Almost any parent can tell you how pleased they are when they hear from a teacher that their child has been a good student in the classroom, kind and generous to other children, making an effort to obey classroom rules. Most parents don't expect to hear that their child is perfect, but it's affirming to hear that one's child is doing his or her best in all areas of classroom life.

In a similar way, knowing we've made a faithful, sincere effort to obey God (doing what is right and showing love to others) gives us the assurance that we belong to the truth. If we're not even trying—or if we believe our behavior doesn't matter, then "the truth is not in us" (1:8).

How Do We Know God Lives In Us?
John puts a caboose on his train of thought in this passage as he tells how we can know that God lives in us. If our own hearts do not condemn us (sometimes described as pangs of conscience), we will have confidence when we approach God, and we will receive from the Lord anything we ask (3:21-22). Why will we have this confidence and see these results? "Because we obey [God's] commands and do what pleases him" (3:22). Again, it's in the doing that we see God's work in us, God's presence in us, revealed.

"And this is [God's] command: to believe in the name of his Son, Jesus Christ, and to love one another as he commanded us" (3:23). That's it. It's that easy to summarize—if we believe in Jesus and love each other, God lives in us. We know this because God confirms it "by the Spirit he gave" to live in us (3:24).

And how do we know it's God's Spirit? That's the topic John discusses next, in our next lesson.

Additional Notes

3:1—Most English versions of the Bible (including the KJV, RSV, and NRSV) refer to the love the Father has "bestowed" on us or "given" us, while the NIV chooses the word "lavished." A danger in this interpretation is that it may mislead readers to think there are different degrees of the Father's love, that God merely *gives* it to some while *lavishing* it on others.

3:21-22—John further explains the believer's confidence before God in 5:14-15: "This is the confidence we have in approaching God: that if we ask anything according to his will, he hears us. And if we know that he hears us—whatever we ask—we know that we have what we asked of him." The phrase "according to his will" makes clear that we may not expect God to respond to frivolous requests in prayer.

GENERAL DISCUSSION

1. Take a few moments to discuss the term "children of God." How does this term describe us differently than do terms such as "servants of God" or "subjects of God"?

2. John assures us that when Jesus returns, we will be like him. (See Rom. 8:29 for a similar teaching by the apostle Paul.) John then says that "everyone who has this hope in [Jesus] purifies" oneself (3:3). How is this possible? What does it mean to purify ourselves in anticipation of Christ's return?

LESSON 5: THIS IS HOW WE KNOW

3. Since everyone sins and breaks the law, how can John say, "He who does what is right is righteous," and, "He who does what is sinful is of the devil" (1 John 3:7-8)? What does John mean? Why does he use visible behavior as the test for who belongs to God and who belongs to the devil?

4. Why does John use the example of Cain and Abel (1 John 3:12)? What does this example teach us about the world's attitude toward us, and about Jesus' command for us to "love one another" (John 13:34-35; 1 John 3:11)?

5. How does doing what pleases God give us confidence before God? In light of this, can we really expect to receive from God anything we ask? Why or why not?

SMALL GROUP SESSION IDEAS

Opening (10-15 minutes)

Prayer—In Psalm 139 King David reminds us of how perfectly God knows everything about us, and in this lesson we're focusing on how we can know more about God and what God desires from us. Begin your opening prayer with verses 1-16 of the psalm, and ask God to use this lesson to help all of you grow in the knowledge we need to be obedient to God's Word.

Share—If you decided to try the fund-raising auction project (the group project suggestion in lesson 4), give a brief update on its progress. Some of you also might like to talk about a simpler living decision you've made (in response to last session's Goalsetting suggestion).

Focus—Again and again John points out that our nature is revealed by our actions. Keep these questions in mind throughout this session: *What do my actions reveal about my nature? Are my words and deeds consistent with what I believe about myself?*

Growing (30-35 minutes)

Read—You may wish to read through the Scripture for this session before moving into your discussion time. As you do, note how often John uses a form of the word *know*.

Discuss—This can be a difficult passage to understand, and we have to be careful not to lift some of John's statements out of context. For each of the General Discussion questions, you may want to look again at the text and read exactly what John says on the subject. After reviewing the General Discussion material, choose from among the following questions to add to your application of the lesson material.

- What are some of the best things about belonging to the family you were raised in? What does it mean to you to be a member of this family? What does this teach us about belonging to God's family?

- Since Jesus paid the price for all our sins (1 John 2:2; 3:5), why does it matter whether or not we continue to sin? Why should we work so hard at something we can't do perfectly?

- What are some of the influences that are trying to lead us astray in our time? Which are the most tempting and treacherous, and how can we defend ourselves against them?

- John says we should not be surprised if the world hates us (1 John 3:13). Should we be surprised or concerned if the world doesn't hate us? Explain.

- What are some ways in which you have observed people laying down their lives for others?

- Believe in Jesus, and love one another (1 John 3:23). Can the Christian life really be this simple? Explain.

Goalsetting (5 minutes)

John encourages us to be aware of various ways in which we are being tempted to go astray. Make it a goal to keep a daily journal between now and the next session, taking note of people and/or experiences that seek to draw you toward the world and away from God. Be prepared to discuss a few examples at your next meeting.

Closing (10 minutes)

Preparing for Prayer—Share prayer requests about any joys or concerns you might have, especially with regard to topics discussed during this session.

Prayer—Read Psalm 139:23-24 to open your closing prayer, and ask God to help all of you with the work of obedience and remembering the important things we need to know as we strive to live out our faith, walking as Jesus did. Everyone should feel free as well to join in with prayer requests that have been mentioned.

Group Service Project (Optional)

"Dear children," John writes, "let us not love with words or tongue but with actions and in truth" (1 John 3:18). Many communities have soup kitchens or missions that encourage volunteers to come in and help serve meals and share the good news of Jesus. Consider doing something like this as a group.

What is love, and why do we love?

6

1 JOHN 4

Test the Spirits, Love the Saints

In a Nutshell

John begins this section of his letter by saying a few words about false spirits and the Holy Spirit; then he quickly moves on to the topic of love, returns briefly to the Spirit, and then writes about love again. In what has aptly been called one of the greatest discourses ever written on love, John teaches us in memorable ways that love is both a noun and a verb. Since God is love, and God has shown amazing love for us by sending his Son, we are to embody God's love while putting love into action.

---

1 John 4

¹Dear friends, do not believe every spirit, but test the spirits to see whether they are from God, because many false prophets have gone out into the world. ²This is how you can recognize the Spirit of God: Every spirit that acknowledges that Jesus Christ has come in the flesh is from God, ³but every spirit that does not acknowledge Jesus is not from God. This is the spirit of the antichrist, which you have heard is coming and even now is already in the world.

⁴You, dear children, are from God and have overcome them, because the one who is in you is greater than the one who is in the world. ⁵They are from the world and therefore speak from the viewpoint of the world, and the world listens to them. ⁶We are from God, and whoever knows God listens to us; but whoever is not from God does not listen to us. This is how we recognize the Spirit of truth and the spirit of falsehood.

⁷Dear friends, let us love one another, for love comes from God. Everyone who loves has been born of God and knows God. ⁸Whoever does not love does not know God, because God is love. ⁹This is how God showed his love among us: He sent his one and only Son into the world that we might live through him. ¹⁰This is love: not that we loved God, but that he loved us and sent his Son as an atoning sacrifice for our sins. ¹¹Dear friends, since God so loved us, we also ought to love one another. ¹²No one has ever seen God; but

LESSON 6: TEST THE SPIRITS, LOVE THE SAINTS

if we love one another, God lives in us and his love is made complete in us.

13We know that we live in him and he in us, because he has given us of his Spirit. 14And we have seen and testify that the Father has sent his Son to be the Savior of the world. 15If anyone acknowledges that Jesus is the Son of God, God lives in him and he in God. 16And so we know and rely on the love God has for us.

God is love. Whoever lives in love lives in God, and God in him. 17In this way, love is made complete among us so that we will have confidence on the day of judgment, because in this world we are like him. 18There is no fear in love. But perfect love drives out fear, because fear has to do with punishment. The one who fears is not made perfect in love.

19We love because he first loved us. 20If anyone says, "I love God," yet hates his brother, he is a liar. For anyone who does not love his brother, whom he has seen, cannot love God, whom he has not seen. 21And he has given us this command: Whoever loves God must also love his brother.

Journalism 101

One of the basic rules of journalism is to report the *who, what, when, where, why,* and *how* of any story. If a newly hired journalism graduate wrote a piece omitting any one of these elements, he or she could be sure that the newspaper's editor—not to mention its readers—would be asking about the missing information.

John the evangelist was no cub reporter; he'd been working on the story of Jesus and his love for more than 50 years by the time he wrote this letter we are studying. In spelling out all the essential details of God's astonishing gift of love, John takes us to a different kind of school—teaching us to examine love with an evangelist's eye (more discerning than the most curmudgeonly editor). John didn't want anyone to be fooled by false reports of love. Only God's love could pass John's strict criteria for authenticity.

Who's Your Spirit?

Chapter 4 opens with a continuation of John's thinking expressed at the end of the previous section of his letter. John was writing about how we can know that God dwells in us, saying, "We know it by the Spirit he gave us" (1 John 3:24). This thought appears to have triggered a concern in his mind about false spirits.

So John continues: "Dear friends, do not believe every spirit, but test the spirits to see whether they are from God, because many false prophets have gone out into the world" (4:1). Almost anyone can step in front of a crowd and proclaim, "I have a message from God!" (This calls to mind a story in which a man calls his minister on Sunday morning and says, "The Lord just told me I'm supposed to speak to the congregation

55

today!" to which the minister replies, "That's funny; I was just talking to him too, and he didn't mention anything to me about that!")

There were many false prophets in John's day who claimed to have messages from the Lord. If they possessed even a little charisma, they could probably persuade a group of believers that they were onto something unique, some special knowledge that no one else had heard from God. (Remember that the claim to special knowledge was at the heart of Gnosticism.)

This technique of false teachers continues to be popular today. In North America alone, there are many individuals and groups—several of which are known for door-to-door evangelism—who proclaim their own unique message, allegedly received from the Lord as an addition to Holy Scripture. Some proclaim the teachings of a leader who claimed to have received a divine visitation or special revelation; others claim that they themselves are the conduits of divine communication.

John proposed a test for such teachers that is as fitting today as it was at the turn of the first century: "This is how you can recognize the Spirit of God: Every spirit that acknowledges that Jesus Christ has come in the flesh is from God, but every spirit that does not acknowledge Jesus is not from God" (4:2-3). The basis of many heresies is the denial of either the divinity or humanity of Jesus Christ.

Those who denied Jesus' divinity said that Jesus was a really good man, a great prophet, or perhaps even someone who was temporarily inhabited by the Spirit of God, but they denied that he was truly and eternally God. Note Jesus' teaching about himself in John 14:11, however: "Believe me when I say that I am in the Father and the Father is in me."

At the same time, there were other teachers who denied that Jesus was ever human. They alleged that he only "appeared" to be human but never took on real human flesh and blood. John's report in his gospel account, however, makes it clear that "the Word became flesh and made his dwelling among us" (John 1:14). As we've noted in earlier lessons, one significant consequence of the denial that Jesus was human was the belief that the body—and anything else made of physical matter—was of no account, while the human spirit was of utmost importance.

So, in line with John's test for heresy, we should ask, *What do the members of any particular group believe about Jesus?* If the response is consistent with what God's Word has revealed about Jesus Christ, their teaching may be trustworthy (see 1 Cor. 12:3). But if their teaching denies the human or divine personhood of Jesus, it is a false teaching.

Knowing the Enemy
John didn't want anyone to take false teachers lightly—another good reminder in our time, when tolerance of every point of view is far more popular than defending biblical truth. "This is the spirit of the antichrist, which you have heard is coming and even now is already in the world" (1 John 4:3). If followers of the truth remain silent in the face of false teaching, the spirit of the antichrist will continue to deceive the world (see "Antifellowship, Antitruth, Antichrists" in lesson 4).

John assured his readers, however, that these false spirits would not conquer them. "You, dear children, are from God and have overcome them, because the one who is in you is greater than the one who is in the world" (4:4).

As good as this news is for believers, it leaves us with a deep concern for and about people who are "from the world." John says that false teachers who are from the world "speak from the viewpoint of the world, and the world listens to them" (4:5). We see evidence of this everywhere in our contemporary society. Some days it seems as if everything that comes from the world—secular music, movies, fashion, TV, books, magazines—speaks more clearly than what comes from God. The church has a hard time getting the world's attention.

People who are from God, however, speak from God's point of view, and "whoever knows God listens" (4:6). It's important to remember that John's main concern in this part of his letter is for faithful believers, people who are from God, many of whom have been beginning to listen to people who are from the world. In other words, John isn't writing to convince unbelievers to turn to God as much as he is writing to caution believers from turning to the world.

Who, What, When, Where, Why, How
John next explains that God's viewpoint is all about love. What this means in logical terms is that if we are from God and if love is from God, then showing love is the obvious way to demonstrate that we are from God. What John says, precisely, is "Dear friends, let us love one another, for love comes from God" (4:7). And in the verses that follow, John answers the journalist's who, what, when, where, why, and how questions about love.

Who is love? "God is love" (4:8, 16). Love isn't simply a human emotion or an occasional burst of passion between people; love is the very essence of the One who created us. It would take countless pages of writing to fully examine the significance of this fact, what it means in terms of God's creative power, providence, justice, and more. Just the implications for our relationships with God and with each other could fill several books, but in the end nothing we can say is as profound or complete as John's simple declaration "God is love." This is how God has chosen to reveal himself to us.

What is love? "This is how God showed his love among us: He sent his one and only Son into the world that we might live through him" (4:10). John's answer about the nature of love focuses on the example of God's sacrifice on our behalf. God's only Son came to fulfill the requirements of love on our behalf. In this act of sacrifice we see God's deep concern for us in this world and God's desire to enjoy our fellowship in the world to come. "This is love," John said, "not that we loved God, but that he loved us and sent his Son as an atoning sacrifice for our sins" (4:10).

When is love? This question is a little trickier. On the one hand, since we now know that God is love, we also know that love exists eternally. On the other hand, we see specific examples of love in action whenever we see people living out God's command to love one another. "No one has ever seen God," John says, reminding us that there's a lot about God's nature that we can't always see, "but if we love one another, God lives in us and his love is made complete in us" (4:12). In other words, our love for each other demonstrates to the world that love is always present, both in God and in the people—the body of Christ—in whom God dwells. God confirms this for us through his Holy Spirit: "We know that we live in him and he in us, because he has given us of his Spirit" (4:13).

Where is love? The easy answer to this question is "Everywhere!" Wherever God is, love is—and God is present everywhere. But John answers this question by narrowing the focus to where we see the greatest love in action. "We have seen and testify that the Father has sent his Son to be the Savior of the world. If anyone acknowledges that Jesus is the Son of God, God lives in him and he in God" (4:15-16). In other words, the love so evident in Jesus is also now present in all who believe in him. We find love wherever we find Jesus and his followers. (See also John 13:34-35.)

LESSON 6: TEST THE SPIRITS, LOVE THE SAINTS

Why is there love? Many journalists have a hard time with "why" questions. Whenever a newsworthy event takes place, whether it's an accident, a crime, or a surprising act of mercy, the author will often write, "The cause is under investigation," or, "The motive is unknown."

John offers several answers to the "why" question about love. While we may not be able to answer fully *why* God loves us, aside from the fact that we are God's creatures made in God's image, John helps us see clearly why God *shows* his love to us. God shows us amazing love in Christ so that we can be saved from sin (4:10, 14) and "live through him" (4:9) and even live "in God" with God living in us (4:13, 16). "In this way, love is made complete among us *so that* we will have confidence on the day of judgment, because in this world we are like him" (4:17). To say that love is made complete among us means that the purpose of God's love is fulfilled—and that includes making us to be "like him," the purpose for which we are created in God's image.

God also gives us love in order to drive out fear. "There is no fear in love. But perfect love drives out fear, because fear has to do with punishment. The one who fears is not made perfect in love" (4:18). The world confronts us with countless reasons to be afraid of everything from war and terrorism to disease and disaster. But people who have received God's love and show love to each other know that they ultimately have nothing to fear. They know God's love has removed their punishment for sin.

Further, we love God and each other because God first loved us (4:19). Our love is always in response to God; it is only because of God's love that we are even able to love.

As we look at the last main question the journalist must try to answer—*How?*—we can see that we've already touched on how love works and how God shows love. But how do we show that God's love is in us? John answers quite simply: "Whoever loves God must also love his brother" (4:21). As John has indicated several times before, it's impossible to love God and hate others. If we are loved, we in turn will show love. In fact, faithfully loving others will eventually answer all of our who, what, when, where, why, and how questions about God's amazing gift of love.

Additional Notes
4:5—Jesus makes a similar point in John's gospel account: "If you belonged to the world, it would love you as its own. As

it is, you do not belong to the world, but I have chosen you out of the world. That is why the world hates you" (John 15:19).

4:8, 16—It's important to remember that John says, "God is love," not "love is God," as some people surmise. We worship not the idea of love but the author of love. Far too often we mistake the human emotion—which is also easily confused with infatuation, romance, or even lust—for the divine gift. The world readily worships every kind of false, human love but rarely acknowledges the self-giving, unconditional love that comes only from God.

The Bible uses several different terms for love. In the original Greek, they are *eros*, which we know as physical or erotic love; *phileo*, which is the love of friendship or companionship, often called "brotherly love"; and *agape*, the mature, all-encompassing desire for the well-being of another person, with no strings attached. John and other New Testament writers use this last term to describe God's love.

GENERAL DISCUSSION

1. What does John mean when he says, "Test the spirits to see whether they are from God" (1 John 4:1)? Where were these spirits found? What effect were ungodly spirits having on the churches? How can we recognize the Spirit of God?

2. John teaches us that love comes from God (1 John 4:7). How does God's love compare with the world's concept of love? What examples of both godly love and worldly love can you think of?

3. Why is it impossible to receive God's love and not show love for our brothers, sisters, and others (1 John 4:20)? How does loving one another make God's love complete in us (4:12)? How does it make God's love visible to the world?

LESSON 6: TEST THE SPIRITS, LOVE THE SAINTS

4. What evidence does John offer to give us "confidence on the day of judgment" (1 John 4:17)? What does John mean when he says "there is no fear in love" and "perfect love drives out fear" (4:18)?

5. In what ways are John's ideals in this chapter attainable?

SMALL GROUP SESSION IDEAS

Opening (10-15 minutes)
Prayer—Before opening with prayer, you may wish to read 1 Corinthians 13, which is often described as a "love chapter" in the Bible (like 1 John 4). After the reading, quietly ask God for the gift of a more loving spirit. Then close by asking God to use this study time to more clearly reveal his love.

Share—If any of you kept a journal as suggested for Goalsetting during the previous session, how many people, places, or things did you notice that tried to turn you toward the world and away from God? Make a list of responses, placing checkmarks next to repeated items (for example, television). Keep the list posted during the rest of this session to serve as a reminder of things we're up against each day as we strive for a loving attitude toward others. (You can do this exercise even if no one kept a journal; simply list things that are most likely to distract you or draw you away from God.)

Focus—Keep these two questions in mind throughout the discussion of this lesson: *How has God revealed his love in my life? How have I shown that love to others?*

Growing (30-35 minutes)
Read—The Scripture for this lesson is one of those chapters of the Bible that benefits from a dramatic reading. If someone in the group has excellent dramatic reading skills, perhaps he or she would like to read 1 John 4 while the rest of the group simply listens. Afterward talk about any details you noticed or insights you gained that might have come across in new way through this reading.

Discuss—The General Discussion questions are written to help sharpen our understanding of the text. Begin with those and include some or all of the following additional questions as you seek to apply John's teaching in your everyday living.

- What is the world's viewpoint (1 John 4:5) on subjects such as money, relationships, entertainment, justice, and worship? What subjects would you add to this list, and why? Why are people quick to listen to the world's viewpoint?

- Why is it significant to note that God loved us before we loved God (1 John 4:10-11, 19)? Should we wait for others to love us before we love them? What implications does this have for evangelism? Relief work? Worship?

- What do you think people fear most about the day of judgment? Why? How should we respond to people who try to take advantage of these fears?

Goalsetting (5 minutes)

The goal for this session is easy to say but hard to do. Think of a person whom you find hard to love. Make it a goal between now and the next session is to take one concrete step toward loving that person. (This is not something that has to be reported on at the next session.)

Closing (10 minutes)

Preparing for Prayer—Review: What are some specific concerns we can pray about in light of John's teachings in the passage for this lesson? Also mention any personal praises or concerns you may wish to share.

Prayer—Read John 21:15-17. Then, as a group, offer brief prayers about the various praises and concerns that have been raised. Ask the Lord to give all of you the strength to remain firm in faith and to keep trying to live by God's love and show it to others.

Here's how we can be sure . . .

7

1 JOHN 5

Faithful Witnesses

In a Nutshell

In the final chapter of his first letter John tells his readers how they can know they are born of God, how they can show their love for God and for all God's children, and how they can be certain Jesus is the Son of God. John then closes with several last-minute thoughts: about eternal life, prayer, sins that lead to death (and sins that don't), living under God's control or the world's, and keeping away from idols—all in 21 verses!

1 John 5

[1]Everyone who believes that Jesus is the Christ is born of God, and everyone who loves the father loves his child as well. [2]This is how we know that we love the children of God: by loving God and carrying out his commands. [3]This is love for God: to obey his commands. And his commands are not burdensome, [4]for everyone born of God overcomes the world. This is the victory that has overcome the world, even our faith. [5]Who is it that overcomes the world? Only he who believes that Jesus is the Son of God.

[6]This is the one who came by water and blood—Jesus Christ. He did not come by water only, but by water and blood. And it is the Spirit who testifies, because the Spirit is the truth. [7]For there are three that testify: [8]the Spirit, the water and the blood; and the three are in agreement. [9]We accept man's testimony, but God's testimony is greater because it is the testimony of God, which he has given about his Son.

[10]Anyone who believes in the Son of God has this testimony in his heart. Anyone who does not believe God has made him out to be a liar, because he has not believed the testimony God has given about his Son. [11]And this is the testimony: God has given us eternal life, and this life is in his Son. [12]He who has the Son has life; he who does not have the Son of God does not have life.

[13]I write these things to you who believe in the name of the Son of God so that you may know that you have eternal life. [14]This is the confidence we have in approaching God: that if we ask anything according to his will, he hears us. [15]And if we know that he hears us—whatever we ask—we know that we have what we asked of him.

[16]If anyone sees his brother commit a sin that does not lead to death, he should pray and God will give him life. I refer to those whose sin does not lead to death. There is a sin that leads to death. I am not saying that he should pray about that.

[17]All wrongdoing is sin, and there is sin that does not lead to death.

[18]We know that anyone born of God does not continue to sin; the one who was born of God keeps him safe, and the evil one cannot harm him. [19]We know that we are children of God, and that the whole world is under the control of the evil one.

[20]We know also that the Son of God has come and has given us understanding, so that we may know him who is true. And we are in him who is true—even in his Son Jesus Christ. He is the true God and eternal life.

[21]Dear children, keep yourselves from idols.

Step by Step

While trying out a new recipe from an unfamiliar cookbook, I missed an important step in the instructions. I had added several ingredients too soon, and there was no way to remove them and correct my mistake without making a huge mess, wasting a lot of food, or starting over from scratch—not to mention making my family wait another hour for supper! The final result was edible, but I was disappointed with myself for missing that key step. Until I try that recipe again, I'll wonder how much better it could have been.

In a similar way (sort of), John the apostle wants to help first-century believers avoid disappointment—or, worse yet, disaster. He gives them step-by-step instructions for making their churches the best they can be.

Step 1: Make sure all the people who are part of the church are "born of God." How can church leaders be sure of that? "Everyone who believes that Jesus is the Christ is born of God," John declares (1 John 5:1). As Jesus once told Nicodemus, a person is "born again" when he or she believes that Jesus is God's only Son, sent to save the world (John 3:3, 16). This is what it means to believe that Jesus is the Christ.

If we review what John says about false teachings in this letter, we'll clearly see that believing in Jesus is not an optional ingredient in John's recipe for a strong, faithful church; neither is any substitution allowed. Church members who did not believe in both the full humanity and full divinity of Jesus were not born of God and would only serve to create an unacceptable mix in the Lord's church.

Step 2: Understand that people who are born of God will love not only their Father but also his children. "Everyone who loves the father loves his child as well" (5:1). In this statement "child" refers not only to Jesus but also to all people who show themselves to be "born of God" by believing in Jesus. A church that consists of people who love God or Jesus but who can't get along with each other can hardly be considered a true church.

LESSON 7: FAITHFUL WITNESSES

Something has gone seriously wrong in their understanding of God's love and how Jesus' followers are being shaped to act.

If that has happened, maybe they've disregarded *step 3:* "This is how we know that we love the children of God: by loving God and carrying out his commands" (5:2). We show our love for God and for others by obeying the commandments God has given us. These are commonly summarized in the Ten Commandments (Ex. 20:1-17), and a helpful teaching by Jesus himself points out that all of God's law hangs on these two summary commands: "Love the Lord your God with all your heart and with your soul and with all your mind" and "Love your neighbor as yourself" (Matt. 22:37-40). We cannot do one without the other, and we cannot break one without violating the other. As James explains, if we break any part of the law, we break the whole law (James 2:10). (See also Mic. 6:8 for another helpful summary of God's law.) To ignore God's commandments not only shows a lack of respect for our Father's wisdom but also demonstrates a sinful superiority on our part, as if the commandments are for other, less enlightened people.

John wants to make sure that no one is inadvertently guilty of this error. So in no uncertain terms he says, "This is love for God: to obey his commands" (5:3).

Recall again that false teachers were playing fast and loose with scriptural teachings about sin and obedience. Their assertion was that sins of the flesh didn't matter (again, as we consider our own society, it's easy to see why this was a popular heresy). Some years earlier, the apostle Paul had to deal with a similar problem: "What then? Shall we sin because we are not under law but under grace? By no means! Don't you know that when you offer yourselves to someone to obey him as slaves, you are slaves to the one whom you obey—whether you are slaves to sin, which leads to death, or to obedience, which leads to righteousness?" (Rom. 6:15-16). Neither John nor Paul—nor Jesus, for that matter—wanted anyone to think the gift of salvation did away with the need to obey God's law (see Matt. 5:17-20).

Just as a cookbook will sometimes include a word of encouragement to the chef ("Try this dish; it's not as difficult as it seems"), so John includes an encouraging word for his readers: "And [God's] commands are not burdensome, for everyone born of God overcomes the world. This is the victory that has overcome the world, even our faith" (5:3-4). We really can do this, John is saying. God's gift of faith not only enables us to believe in Jesus but also gives us the ability to be obedient in the face of worldly temptations. And as the product of faith, this same obedience proves to be the key ingredient in John's recipe for a victorious church: "Who is it that overcomes the world? Only he who believes that Jesus is the Son of God" (5:5).

If we skip any of these steps—believing, loving, obeying—the church simply won't turn out right in the end!

The Whole Truth and Nothing but the Truth

By now it's clear that the key to everything John has been saying in his letter—about light and darkness, new and old commands, loving God and loving the world, obedience and disobedience—is Jesus Christ. If Jesus Christ is who he claims to be, everything else falls into place. But if he isn't, the false teachers may deserve a hearing.

In line with Old Testament teaching (Deut. 19:15; see also Matt. 18:16), John offered three witnesses to confirm his testimony: water, blood, and the Holy Spirit. The water represents Jesus' baptism; the blood represents Jesus' crucifixion; and the Holy Spirit is God's own testimony in the hearts of God's people.

At Jesus' baptism the Holy Spirit descended and lighted on Jesus like a dove, and a voice spoke from heaven, saying, "This is my Son, whom I love; with him I am well pleased" (see Matt. 3:16-17). In his gospel acount John was even more deliberate in explaining what this meant:

> Then John [the Baptist] gave this testimony: "I saw the Spirit come down from heaven as a dove and remain on him. I would not have known him, except that the one who sent me to baptize with water told me, 'The man on whom you see the Spirit come down and remain is he who will baptize with the Holy Spirit.' I have seen and I testify that this is the Son of God." (John 1:32-34)

Jesus' crucifixion similarly revealed him to be God's Son. Matthew recorded the words of people who could at best be considered impartial witnesses: "When the centurion and those with him who were guarding Jesus saw the earthquake and all that had happened, they were terrified, and exclaimed, 'Surely he was the Son of God!'" (Matt. 27:54). Mark and Luke noted similar testimonies (Mark 15:39; Luke 23:47), and John added this explanation:

> When they came to Jesus and found that he was already dead, they did not break his legs. Instead, one of the soldiers pierced Jesus' side with a spear,

> bringing a sudden flow of blood and water. The man who saw it has given testimony, and his testimony is true. He knows that he tells the truth, and he testifies so that you also may believe. These things happened so that the scripture would be fulfilled: "Not one of his bones will be broken," and, as another scripture says, "They will look on the one they have pierced." (John 19:33-37)

In baptism and crucifixion, the water and the blood testified that Jesus was the Son of God. And in each of these events people testified that this was true ("man's testimony").

As persuasive as John considered the testimony about the water and the blood to be, he knew there was another witness who was even more convincing: "We accept man's testimony, but God's testimony is greater because it is the testimony of God, which he has given about his Son" (5:9). This testimony, that of the Holy Spirit, is also the easiest to find. "Anyone who believes in the Son of God has this testimony in his heart" (5:10).

To deny this testimony is to call God a liar, John asserts (5:10). As he wrote these words, John may have been thinking of Jesus' words at the Last Supper: "If you love me, you will obey what I command. And I will ask the Father, and he will give you another Counselor to be with you forever—the Spirit of truth. The world cannot accept him, because it neither sees him nor knows him. But you know him, for he lives with you and will be in you" (John 14:15-17). Notice how everything John has been saying is wrapped up in Jesus' words—love, obedience, Spirit, truth. None of these ideas was John's own. As John said at the very beginning of the letter, "That which was from the beginning, which we have heard, which we have seen with our eyes, which we have looked at and our hands have touched—this we proclaim concerning the Word of life" (1 John 1:1). John was simply being a faithful witness.

Just One More Thing, or Maybe Two or Three
Though John has completed his thoughts about belief, love, and obedience, as well as the testimony of the Spirit, the water, and the blood, he still has a few more things to pass along. He begins with a word of explanation about why he is writing (similar to what we find in John 20:31): "I write these things to you who believe in the name of the Son of God so that you may know that you have eternal life" (1 John 5:13).

It may be that the worst thing a false teacher can do is sow doubt about something that previously has been a comforting assurance. By saying there was special knowledge required for salvation, or that Jesus wasn't who he claimed to be, false teachers were causing some members of the church to second-guess their faith. So John was writing to assure them that what they had learned about eternal life from the beginning was true.

To further assure his readers, John again refers to something Jesus said: "If you remain in me and my words remain in you, ask whatever you wish, and it will be given you" (John 15:7). Echoing this thought, John says, "This is the confidence we have in approaching God: that if we ask anything according to his will, he hears us. And if we know that he hears us—whatever we ask—we know that we have what we asked of him" (1 John 5:14-15). This includes eternal life, no matter what false teachers might be saying.

Still thinking about eternal life, John's thoughts turn briefly to the subject of sin. Is it possible to lose the promise of eternal life because of sin? In a much-debated passage, John says there are some sins that do not lead to death, so we should pray for people who commit such sins, asking God to give them life (5:16). But "there is a sin that leads to death," John says, and he adds that he is not saying we should pray for people who are guilty of that sin.

The gospel of Mark gives us some insight into this "sin that leads to death." Jesus said, "I tell you the truth, all sins and blasphemies of men will be forgiven them. But whoever blasphemes against the Holy Spirit will never be forgiven; he is guilty of an eternal sin" (Mark 3:28-29). Note also what John says earlier in this chapter about anyone who does not believe the testimony of God in his or her heart, making God out to be a liar (1 John 5:10). This seems to fit the description of a person who "blasphemes against the Holy Spirit."

While we cannot know whether John was familiar with the book of Hebrews, we can say he would have agreed with its author regarding persons who had once belonged to the church but who were now teaching a false gospel:

> It is impossible for those who have once been enlightened, who have tasted the heavenly gift, who have shared in the Holy Spirit, who have tasted the goodness of the word of God and the powers of the coming age, if they fall away, to be brought back to repentance, because to their loss they are crucify-

LESSON 7: FAITHFUL WITNESSES

ing the Son of God all over again and subjecting him to public disgrace. (Heb. 6:4-6)

From this description we can begin to understand why John says there is "a sin that leads to death" while there are other sins that can be forgiven.

This Is What We Know

John concludes his letter with a brief review of the things he wants every believer to know: *First,* "that anyone born of God does not continue to sin" (1 John 5:18)—that is, makes every effort to resist sin (see discussion of 1:8-9 in lesson 2). *Second,* "we know that we are children of God" even though the world "is under the control of the evil one" (5:19). *Third,* "we know also that the Son of God has come and has given us understanding, so that we may know him who is true" (5:20; see 5:10-12). What's more, we are even "in him who is true," so God's love is made complete among us and we can live in complete confidence that we belong forever to Christ, "the true God and eternal life" (5:20; see 4:15-18).

Finally, seemingly out of left field, John says, "Dear children, keep yourselves from idols." Though John has not said a word about idols before this point, the teachings being promoted by false teachers were essentially idol worship. They tempted the people to abandon the truth of the gospel in order to follow a new, selfish, self-indulgent, disobedient teaching, which is idol worship of the worst kind. No deity of human imagination can ever substitute for the one true God of heaven who sent his Son to be our Savior.

Additional Notes

5:2-3—John uses two different action words for keeping God's commandments. We are to *carry out* God's commands, and we are to *obey* them. In the original Greek text, the first of these terms conveys the sense of dutifully doing whatever the commandments require, while the second carries a sense of appreciating or even cherishing the commandments. For John, love and keeping God's Word always go hand in hand.

5:7-10—In combination with the Spirit, the water, and the blood, John identifies human testimony, God's testimony, and the inner testimony of the Holy Spirit ("testimony in [one's] heart") as witnesses to the truth about Jesus.

5:19—Keep in mind John's distinction throughout this letter concerning people who have fellowship with God and those who are of the world. When John says that "the whole world is under the control of the evil one," he is not referring to those whose allegiance is with God.

GENERAL DISCUSSION

1. When we are "born of God" (1 John 5:1), we become a part of God's family. Who else is in this family? How should we treat family members? Are there any exceptions? How do God's commands help us demonstrate love for God's entire family?

2. Do you agree with John's assessment that God's commands are not burdensome (1 John 5:3)? What would most people say? What has God given to help us in keeping his commands rather than following the way of the world?

3. How did the baptism and crucifixion of Jesus identify him as the Christ, the Son of God? How does the Holy Spirit confirm this identity? Of the "three that testify" (1 John 5:7), which do you think is most persuasive? Which is most useful in teaching others about the identity of Jesus?

4. What are some examples of sins that either do or do not lead to spiritual death? What does John tell us our response should be in each of these situations? Does John prohibit prayer in either situation?

5. After his encouraging recital of all the things we know for certain (1 John 5:18-20), John's last word in this letter is about idols. Why?

LESSON 7: FAITHFUL WITNESSES

SMALL GROUP SESSION IDEAS

Opening (10-15 minutes)

Note together that this lesson is about the faithful witnesses God has provided to assure us that Jesus is the Christ and that we have already received the promised gift of eternal life. Emphasize that God's witnesses are in perfect agreement; their testimony about Jesus is sure.

Prayer—Before opening with prayer, read John 15:1-8, paying special attention to God's promise to grant whatever we ask (15:7) in line with God's will, a promise that John repeats in our Scripture for this lesson (see 1 John 5:14). Then pray together, asking God to use this time of study to make all of us better witnesses for Jesus' sake.

Share—Since this is our last lesson on the content of John's first letter, you may wish to discuss any lingering questions you might have from previous lessons. Or you may wish to talk more about the role of being witnesses. Maybe some members of the group have served on juries or even given eyewitness testimony in a trial. If so, what was the experience like? Did you find it easy or hard to give a truthful report of what you had experienced?

Focus—The Scripture for this lesson covers a lot of material, but at its center is the role of God's faithful witnesses. Without these, especially the Holy Spirit within us, we would have no confidence about Jesus as Savior and Lord. As you work through this lesson, keep this question in mind: *How is God using John's testimony to give me greater confidence of faith?*

Growing (30-35 minutes)

Read—Read 1 John 5 together, emphasizing that there are two main sections—5:1-12 and 5:13-21—by having a different person read each one.

Discuss—The Scripture for this lesson has enough thought-provoking material for many hours of discussion, so you may have to pick just a few of the General Discussion questions to discuss at length. Choose also from among the following questions, or supply some of your own, for additional application of the lesson material.

- Among all the children of God, whom do you find hardest to love? Why? Is it helpful to think about simply keeping God's commandments as a way of showing love? Explain.

- The testimony in the Bible about Jesus' baptism and crucifixion has been handed down unchanged for more than two thousand years. In your opinion, does this make it more or less credible? Why? What role does the Spirit play in convincing you of the truthfulness of God's witnesses?
- If you could talk to one person who encountered Jesus firsthand during his public ministry, who would it be? What would you ask him or her?
- When you pray, are you convinced that God hears and will grant you whatever you ask? Why or why not?
- Give some examples to show that "the whole world is under the control of the evil one" (1 John 5:19). How does God keep us safe? Since even deeply committed Christians suffer the consequences of sin, what does John mean when he says the evil one cannot harm us?
- Which contemporary idols pose the greatest threat to the church today? Explain.

Goalsetting (5 minutes)

Although there are many personal goals we could pursue as a result of John's teaching in this chapter—such as loving God's children, obeying God's commands, and believing God's witnesses—perhaps it would be most helpful to set a goal of listening to the testimony of God's Spirit. Most of us spend so little time in silence just listening for God that we may often be ignoring the direction of the Spirit in our hearts.

Between now and the next session, make an effort to set aside time for listening to God. Maybe this will mean turning off the radio or TV, or taking a walk in silence. Whatever form your listening takes, begin by telling God that you are ready to hear; then pay close attention to the thoughts God brings to mind.

In connection with this, consider memorizing the first two verses of our passage for this lesson (1 John 5:1-2). These verses provide an apt summary of John's letter and give us a concise explanation of the gospel message and how God wants us to live.

Closing (10 minutes)

Preparing for Prayer—Return to John 15 to read verses 9-12. What are we promised before we even turn to God in our prayers? Also mention any concerns or praises you might wish to share.

LESSON 7: FAITHFUL WITNESSES

Prayer—As you pray, include requests for greater love, greater obedience, and greater confidence in faith. Everyone should feel free to join in, bringing each other's petitions and praises to the Lord.

Group Study Project (Optional)
In preparation for studying John's second letter, in which the apostle uses the word "truth" five times in just the first few sentences, do some research on the concept of truth in God's Word. Using a concordance or a Bible dictionary, look up two or three references to truth. Then prepare to give a brief report at the next session, paying particular attention to these questions: *What was the background of each reference? How did the truth make a difference? How did the truth honor God?*

How can you tell a false teacher from a true one?

8

2 JOHN

Truth or Consequences

In a Nutshell

John's second letter is a brief but powerful essay on the need for truth, love, and persistent faithfulness in the body of Christ. With obvious affection, the apostle/evangelist encourages his beloved Christian friends to continue the course they first began and to guard against anyone who would deceive them into taking new and disastrous directions. John also expresses that he hopes soon to be with his friends to share many more thoughts and to complete their mutual joy.

---

2 John

[1]The elder,

To the chosen lady and her children, whom I love in the truth—and not I only, but also all who know the truth—[2]because of the truth, which lives in us and will be with us forever:

[3]Grace, mercy and peace from God the Father and from Jesus Christ, the Father's Son, will be with us in truth and love.

[4]It has given me great joy to find some of your children walking in the truth, just as the Father commanded us. [5]And now, dear lady, I am not writing you a new command but one we have had from the beginning. I ask that we love one another. [6]And this is love: that we walk in obedience to his commands. As you have heard from the beginning, his command is that you walk in love.

[7]Many deceivers, who do not acknowledge Jesus Christ as coming in the flesh, have gone out into the world. Any such person is the deceiver and the antichrist. [8]Watch out that you do not lose what you have worked for, but that you may be rewarded fully. [9]Anyone who runs ahead and does not continue in the teaching of Christ does not have God; whoever continues in the teaching has both the Father and the Son. [10]If anyone comes to you and does not bring this teaching, do not take him into your house or welcome him. [11]Anyone who welcomes him shares in his wicked work.

[12]I have much to write to you, but I do not want to use paper and ink. Instead, I hope to visit you and talk with you face to face, so that our joy may be complete.

[13]The children of your chosen sister send their greetings.

1, 2, 3 JOHN: LIVING IN THE LIGHT OF LOVE

Sometimes Less Is More

"Okay, class, here's your assignment for tomorrow: I want you to choose a controversial topic, decide on a particular point of view, and write a persuasive essay that will encourage your readers to agree with the perspective you've chosen. Try to include as many convincing arguments as you can; they can be personal, historical, practical, or even emotional. You might also want to describe some of the consequences of not agreeing with your point of view. I also want you to be creative with this. Grab my attention, and don't let it go till you've made your point!

"Oh, and one more thing. I want you keep this to one page, not more than 300 words."

How would you like to be given that kind of assignment? As the person writing this study guide, I'm humbled to realize that just the material for the lesson in this study guide is about ten times as long as John's second letter to his Christian friends—and probably won't say nearly as much! As we can see from John's gospel account, his letters, and the book of Revelation, John had a gift for making a few words speak volumes.

John's topic in this second letter is the same as in his first: the danger of false teachers in the church. John's point of view? Opposed! His persuasive arguments? Knowledge of the truth, love, and obedience. The consequence of believing the opponents' view? Losing the believer's reward in Christ. His attention-getting format? A personal letter.

Obviously John wasn't writing to fulfill an assignment—or was he? Could it be that the Holy Spirit assigned him to grab the attention of the early church—and, down through the centuries, to get a hold of our attention too?

That's My Church

Unlike the first letter attributed to John, this one follows the traditional form for first-century correspondence, similar to what we find in the apostle Paul's letters. First comes the identification of the sender, in this case simply "The elder," and the addressee, here called "the chosen lady and her children" (2 John 1). Next there's usually a salutation, "Grace, mercy and peace . . ." (v. 3), followed by a word of either joy or thanksgiving—in this case, "great joy": "It has given me great joy to find some of your children walking in the truth" (v. 4).

Although the elder does not give his name, he is almost certainly the same author as that of the first and third of these three letters that were always circulated together (see again

LESSON 8: TRUTH OR CONSEQUENCES

"Looking for a Signature" in lesson 1 of this study guide). With a mixture of humility and authority—though he could claim his status as an eyewitness, as in 1 John 1:1-4—John here simply refers to himself as "the elder." It was an appropriate title. John was the elder statesman of the church of Jesus Christ, being most likely the last surviving apostle.

"The chosen lady and her children" are also unidentified. Some scholars suggest that John may have been writing to a specific woman (see Additional Notes), but on the basis of the content and conclusion of this letter, most commentators agree that John was using this title as a term of affection for a particular congregation and its members—and perhaps even for its daughter congregations. "The children of your chosen sister" (2 John 13) can be understood as a reference to one or more congregations, possibly in the region of Ephesus (compare with "she who is in Babylon, chosen together with you"—1 Pet. 5:13—another probable reference to a group of believers).

Truth, Not in Part but the Whole
Though John doesn't specifically identify the "chosen lady," he is not ambiguous about his relationship with her. He loves her "in the truth," as do "all who know the truth" (2 John 1). The reason for this outpouring of love is also spelled out: it's "because of the truth, which lives in us and will be with us forever" (v. 2).

With this affectionate greeting, John introduces two of the major themes of this letter: truth and love. Not surprisingly, they are inseparable. Without truth, there can be no love; and if there is no love, people show they have grossly misunderstood the truth. As John teaches so plainly, those who know the truth and live by the truth obey God's command to love one another.

The particular truth John is writing about is the truth that God has revealed in Jesus Christ. We cannot say it often enough, and we probably can't say it better than John did: "God so loved the world that he gave his one and only Son, that whoever believes in him shall not perish but have eternal life" (John 3:16). To deny this statement or any part of it is to deny God's truth.

Yet that is precisely what false teachers were doing—denying God's truth as revealed in Jesus. Some were denying that Jesus was really God, saying that he only seemed to be divine or that he was only inhabited by the Spirit of God from the time of his baptism (see Matt. 3:16) until his death on the cross ("Father, into your hands I commit my spirit"—Luke 23:46). Others denied that Jesus was ever human, saying that anything consisting of a perfect spirit could not have any contact with sinful, physical matter. In either case, denying any part of the truth about Jesus was a denial of the entire truth about Jesus.

After giving his greeting and salutation, John writes that it has given him "great joy" to find "some . . . children walking in the truth" (2 John 4). We should not attach too much importance to the word "some" here, as if the best John could hope for was to see only a few members of the next generation carrying on the faith. After nearly two millennia, we've come to trust that the Christian faith will be handed on from generation to generation—in fact, we probably expect this more than we expect to see the return of Christ in our lifetime. For John, however, this handing on of the faith was a relatively recent phenomenon, so it wasn't something to be taken for granted (a fitting reminder for us too!).

Love Means Obedience
Believers who know they have been saved by the blood of God's Son know that nothing else matters; the knowledge and assurance of salvation trumps all lesser issues and petty concerns. All of our sins have been forgiven, so we are free to show forgiveness and love even as we have been forgiven and loved. This was the new command Jesus gave to his disciples at the Last Supper. "My command is this: Love each other as I have loved you" (John 15:12).

John knew that if his readers had the whole truth about Jesus in their hearts, they also understood the Lord's command to love each other (2 John 5). And how do Jesus' followers show that love? By obedience to all of God's commands, which false teachers were rejecting.

A proper understanding of what it means to love one another was the centerpiece of John's argument. This continues to be a critical challenge for the church today. "This is love: that we walk in obedience to his commands. As you have heard from the beginning, his command is that you walk in love" (v. 6). Notice how John repeats himself so that there can be no mistaking his meaning: Love demands obedience.

There is no way of knowing whether downplaying obedience to God's law is the most common error made by people who have become Christians, but it must certainly be among the top ten. The assumption is that love does away with law,

LESSON 8: TRUTH OR CONSEQUENCES

but in fact love means we are to embrace God's law. With God, love is obedience and obedience is love. How could disobedience ever be a sign of love?

Yet consider just a few of many signs of disobedience that have become common in today's church. Sabbath observance is rapidly disappearing, regarded by many as quaint or old-fashioned. Believers give all kinds of reasons why we don't really need to keep the Sabbath holy, or set apart for the Lord. But is that what God wants? (A study of what Sabbath is all about could probably benefit many of us, especially if we think it's only about going to worship services on Sunday; see the group study project suggestion at the end of this lesson.)

Using God's name in vain is another violation of God's law that has become so common—and is remarked upon so rarely—that we hardly even notice it anymore. Even if someone's use of Jesus' name as a cuss word gives us pause, how often do we state our objection?

In many ways coveting has become the basis for our economic system, in contrast to the rather outdated model of providing useful goods and services. For example, make a mental list of the reasons why we buy things. How closely do those reasons resemble the reasons portrayed in most advertising? The majority of us eagerly embrace the acquisition of things, making that a much higher priority than the acquisition of a right spirit.

Committing adultery—well, we only have to remember what Jesus said about our eyes and our hearts to know that this is an overwhelming concern (Matt. 5:27-28).

Often we'd like to believe we are committed to obedience, just as the first readers of John's letters might have believed they were walking in the way of love—but the facts simply won't support that belief. We can be thankful that God is merciful and will forgive us "if we confess our sins" (1 John 1:9), but if we disregard God's law or rationalize its importance out of existence, we risk being no different from the false teachers John is writing about.

Don't Be Deceived
A false teacher or teaching can only deceive us if we allow ourselves to be deceived. If we are lacking in either the knowledge of God's truth or the willpower necessary for love and obedience, we are ripe for deception.

John makes clear that false teachers are not a rarity in the church. "Many deceivers, who do not acknowledge Jesus

Christ as coming in the flesh, have gone out into the world. Any such person is the deceiver and the antichrist" (2 John 7). (Recall our earlier discussion of 1 John 2:18-23 on antichrists in lesson 4.)

John hints at a telltale method such deceivers may have been using: "Anyone who runs ahead and does not continue in the teaching of Christ does not have God; whoever continues in the teaching has both the Father and the Son." Perhaps the deceivers were claiming to be advanced thinkers, working "ahead of the curve" or thinking "outside of the box." As much as we've heard these terms in recent years and admired the good that can come with creative thinking and innovation, obedience to God's law is one area in which we want to stay firmly "inside the box," inside the clear boundaries described by God in his Word.

In fact, as John implies, we could use this as a test for false teachers. Is their teaching consistent with God's truth? Do they acknowledge Jesus Christ as the only hope for salvation? Do they demonstrate obedience in their desire to show love? If they fail any of these tests, John says, "Do not take them into your house"—which in those days was not only someone's residence but also the church's meeting place. To offer such deceivers a welcome could give the impression that the church accepts some or all of what they are teaching.

This may sound like a hard teaching. We've been trained to welcome everyone into our churches. But that doesn't mean we have to give everyone an opportunity to teach God's people. For this reason, many churches have developed a system of theological education to train people who will teach in the church, and elders are charged with ensuring that no strange doctrines are taught. So let's be sure to ask, *How carefully are these cautions exercised today? How often do we allow someone to teach simply because they are willing to fill an empty spot in our education programs or pulpits?*

Inadvertent false teachers are one thing; deliberate false teachers pose a calculated threat to the church. A quick review of current religious books, periodicals, and seminar offerings will convince even a fairly new believer that our faith—especially the uniqueness of Jesus Christ—is under attack today. False teachers are relentless, and "anyone who welcomes [them] shares in [their] wicked work" (2 John 11).

LESSON 8: TRUTH OR CONSEQUENCES

Face Time Is Grace Time

A curious phrase in John's parting words serves as a good reminder for all who wish to see the church thrive and grow: "I have much to write to you, but I do not want to use paper and ink" (v. 12). Even though John wrote five of our New Testament books, he knew there was no substitute for personal contact. From the earliest days of the church, believers have spread the good news by talking to one another in person. Paper and ink—or today, digital and video communication—have their place, but "in person" is still the best way to share our joy in Jesus Christ.

John's final greetings also remind us that sister churches can be an encouragement to each other. Whether we are just down the street or on the other side of the world, we all face the same challenges. Believing the truth, walking in love, resisting those who would take us astray—our mutual encouragement can keep us strong in every part of our faith.

Additional Notes

v. 1—Based on the Greek words for "chosen" (*eklecte*) and "lady" (*kyria*), some scholars have suggested that this letter was written to a woman known as "the Lady Electa" or "the elect Kyria." The content of the letter, however, makes it far more likely that it was written to a church.

v. 4—John's rejoicing in having found that some are carrying on the faith may be enhanced in our minds if we note that the original text here uses the word *eureka* (Greek for "I have found").

v. 10—The sense of the original text here is that we are not to give false teachers a reason for rejoicing that their message is acceptable in the church of Christ.

v. 12—The phrase rendered as "talk . . . face to face" is more literally translated as "speak mouth to mouth" to emphasize the value of personal communication over that of "paper and ink."

GENERAL DISCUSSION

1. What truth is John talking about in verses 1-4? Where can we find this truth? How is this kind of truth passed on from generation to generation?

2. Does it seem peculiar to find the words "command" and "love" in the same sentence (2 John 6)? What kind of love would require a command? Is this the same kind of love we receive from God? How is it the same? Different?

3. What does John identify as the false teachers' primary error (2 John 7)? Is this still an issue for the church today? Why or why not? What would you identify as two or three of the most serious errors being taught today, and how are they related to an improper understanding of Jesus?

4. Why does John tell his readers not to welcome false teachers into their house? What harm could have come from welcoming them? How should we apply this instruction today?

5. In John's day a letter could take months or even years to reach its destination, and situations could change dramatically in that amount of time. So face-to-face communication was a treasure. Is such personal communication any less important today? How can we use modern communication tools to make our joy complete?

SMALL GROUP SESSION IDEAS

Opening (10-15 minutes)
Prayer—In light of studying about truth and love in this lesson, consider reading Psalm 25:1-7 together as your opening prayer.

Share—People who worked on the group study project from lesson 7 may wish to report on the "truth" verses they researched. What was the background of each verse? How did the truth make a difference? How did the truth honor God?

LESSON 8: TRUTH OR CONSEQUENCES

Focus—Keep this question in mind throughout this session: *Is my knowledge of the truth and my obedience in love enough to protect me from false teachers?*

Growing (30-35 minutes)

Read—Since the second letter of John is quite brief, consider reading it from one or more different versions or paraphrases, such as *The Message* by Eugene Peterson. How do the different presentations help you notice things you may have missed before in John's message?

Discuss—Begin with the General Discussion questions, which follow John's train of thought in this letter. Then choose from among the following questions as time allows.

- John's reference to himself as "the elder" could have been both a sign of office and a reference to his advancing years. How much respect is given to "the elders" (both kinds) in your church? What danger is there in a church that doesn't listen to its elders?

- In general, do you think believers today have more or less knowledge of the truth than previous generations? Since faith is a free gift from God, why should we care whether people are well-grounded in the truth?

- Do you think you (or your group) could ever come under the influence of a deceiver? What are some of the ways in which that might happen?

- What do antichrists look like? Could we spot one by his or her appearance? If not, what gives them away?

- What do you think John means when he says, "Watch out that you do not lose what you have worked for, but that you may be rewarded fully" (2 John 8)? Was he speaking about this life or the life to come? What are some of the rewards that come from faithfulness? (For other passages written by John and others on "rewards," see Matt. 5:12; John 4:34-38; 1 Cor. 3:8; Rev. 11:18; 22:12.)

Goalsetting (5 minutes)

Nearly every church library offers many excellent resources to help us grow in our knowledge of the truth and to encourage us in our walk of obedience. Consider taking a "field trip" to your church library and each choosing a book to read. You may also wish to give at least a preliminary report on your book at the next session.

Another option could be to look through a few catalogs from Christian booksellers and to order one or more titles for personal study.

Closing (10 minutes)
Preparing for Prayer—Return to Psalm 25 and read verses 8-13, noting the emphasis on truth, obedience, and rewards. What kind of people are guided in what is right? What part does confession play in obedience? After taking a few moments to discuss these matters, share concerns and praises you'd like to bring to the Lord in prayer.

Prayer—As you close this session, keep your Bibles open to Psalm 25, and take turns praying specific verses from the psalm as the Spirit leads. You could also briefly add any other petitions you wish to bring before God. Then close by saying the Lord's Prayer together (see Matt. 6:9-13).

Group Study Project (Optional)
The Goalsetting section above recommends reading different books for personal growth. For a more group-oriented option in light of the next session's being the last in this study, you could all choose to read the same book—such as a novel with a religious theme or an inspirational book on Christian living—and plan on discussing it in future meetings after this study has ended. Bring your suggestions about books to the next meeting.

Group Study Project (Optional)
Some or all of you may be interested in (re)learning about the meaning and purpose of various aspects of God's law, such as honoring the Sabbath, not taking the Lord's name in vain, and so on. Start with the Bible's teaching in Exodus 20 (or Deut. 5) and Matthew 5-7 and consult a major confession such as the Heidelberg Catechism or the Westminster Confession, perhaps looking in commentaries on these Scriptures and confessions as well. Here's a brief list of additional resources that you may find helpful:

- *10 Commandments: Our Guide for Thankful Living* by Joel Kok (Faith Alive, 2002), a Word Alive Bible study; 10 sessions.
- *Catch Your Breath: God's Invitation to Sabbath Rest* by Don Postema (Faith Alive, 1997); 6 sessions.

- *Space for God: Study and Practice of Spirituality and Prayer* (second edition) by Don Postema (Faith Alive, 1997); 10 sessions.

- *Our Only Comfort: A Comprehensive Commentary on the Heidelberg Catechism* by Fred Klooster (Faith Alive, 2001).

For more information or to place an order, visit *www.FaithAliveResources.org* or call toll-free 1-800-333-8300.

Writing to a friend, John teaches about everyday love in action.

3 JOHN

Open Door, Open Heart

In a Nutshell

In contrast to his first two letters, John's third letter is filled with personalities. This is also a more personal letter than the others. The recipient is Gaius, a Christian leader who has been diligent in showing hospitality to traveling evangelists and teachers; John commends him for his faithfulness and love. Two other persons named are Diotrephes, a gossiping church leader who has caused trouble, and Demetrius, a believer who is well spoken of—"even by the truth itself" (3 John 12). From the example of each person mentioned, including the author, we learn important lessons about opening our doors to others and our hearts to God.

---

3 John

¹The elder,

To my dear friend Gaius, whom I love in the truth.

²Dear friend, I pray that you may enjoy good health and that all may go well with you, even as your soul is getting along well. ³It gave me great joy to have some brothers come and tell about your faithfulness to the truth and how you continue to walk in the truth. ⁴I have no greater joy than to hear that my children are walking in the truth.

⁵Dear friend, you are faithful in what you are doing for the brothers, even though they are strangers to you. ⁶They have told the church about your love. You will do well to send them on their way in a manner worthy of God. ⁷It was for the sake of the Name that they went out, receiving no help from the pagans. ⁸We ought therefore to show hospitality to such men so that we may work together for the truth.

⁹I wrote to the church, but Diotrephes, who loves to be first, will have nothing to do with us. ¹⁰So if I come, I will call attention to what he is doing, gossiping maliciously about us. Not satisfied with that, he refuses to welcome the brothers. He also stops those who want to do so and puts them out of the church.

¹¹Dear friend, do not imitate what is evil but what is good. Anyone who does what is good is from God. Anyone who does what is evil has not seen God. ¹²Demetrius is well spoken of by everyone—and even by the truth itself. We also speak well of him, and you know that our testimony is true.

LESSON 9: OPEN DOOR, OPEN HEART

¹³I have much to write you, but I do not want to do so with pen and ink. ¹⁴I hope to see you soon, and we will talk face to face. Peace to you. The friends here send their greetings. Greet the friends there by name.

Postal Pastoring

Having served as a pastor in three different congregations, I could not begin to count the number of letters I've written. Each ministry began with a letter of acceptance and ended with a letter of farewell. In between, there were monthly letters to the congregation, weekly letters to worship visitors, and daily correspondence with colleagues, family, and friends. In addition to these, there were letters to committees and missionaries, letters of recommendation, letters of discipline, and even the occasional letter to our seat of government.

In every case, it wasn't the letter itself that was of any particular value; rather, it was the people involved that made the letters valuable. A letter is nothing more than a piece of paper with words on it, but in the journey from sender to receiver, it becomes a means of communication, of relationship building—and perhaps even an avenue to faith.

Think Globally, Act Locally

John's first letter appears to have been intended for a wide group of readers, perhaps even including all the Christian congregations of his day. It bears no particular greeting or salutation, doesn't mention anyone by name (except to identify the writer), and deals with subjects that were—and continue to be—of universal significance to the church.

The second letter is more narrowly addressed, perhaps to a single congregation or small cluster of congregations (house churches). Its subject matter is also more limited, dealing with truth and love and deceivers who failed to demonstrate a godly understanding of these essential principles for Christian living. Again, no one is mentioned by name.

John's third letter is addressed to an individual Christian leader, Gaius, and the apostle names two other people as well, Diotrephes and Demetrius. Its subject matter is quite specific: John discusses hospitality for traveling missionaries; he mentions a problem that the church is having with Diotrephes; and he puts in a good word for Demetrius, who may well be the person delivering this letter to Gaius. (The apostle Paul makes similar comments in the closing remarks of several letters; see especially Phil. 2:25-30; Col. 4:7-9; Titus 3:12.)

Of all of John's writings this letter seems to be the least intended for general distribution, yet its subject matter, though dealing with a local problem, teaches valuable lessons for the global church.

To Be Like Gaius

Outside of this letter, we know very little about Gaius's identity. The name is a common one and is found elsewhere in the New Testament, but beyond the mention of a gift for hospitality (Rom. 16:23), no direct evidence connects John's Gaius with the other references to people of that name (see also Acts 19:29; 20:4; 1 Cor. 1:14). At best we can guess that the Gaius in 3 John lives somewhere in the province of Asia (modern-day Turkey), since John taught and traveled mainly in that area, according to Clement of Alexandria.

We do, however, know something about Gaius's character, which may be of more value to us than knowing his occupation or where he lived. John wasn't writing to encourage Gaius to change his character in any way—but to stay the course, to keep on being the person he already had become in Christ. So we can say with some confidence that Gaius's example would be a good one for us to follow.

John greets Gaius as a "dear friend" (literally, "beloved," from the Greek *agapeto*) and even adds the description "whom I love in the truth" (3 John 1). This is the same phrase used in the address in 2 John. Since John doesn't offer Gaius any word of explanation about either love or truth, it may be safe to assume that Gaius fully understands what John means by his greeting. This assumption is certainly borne out by Gaius's actions.

Before specifically addressing those actions, John tells Gaius that he has been praying for his friend's health, asking that all will go well with him, even as his soul is getting along well (3 John 2). An important thing to note here is that John isn't making a distinction between the importance of the body and the soul, as if the two could be dealt with separately and unequally—a common error of false teachers in those days and a persistent problem today. If anything, John is drawing attention to the importance of *both* the body and the soul, as is emphasized in 1 Corinthians 15 and 1 Thessalonians 4:13-16 and in church teachings such as the Heidelberg Catechism (see Q&A's 1, 11, 37, 57).

LESSON 9: OPEN DOOR, OPEN HEART

An Open-Door Policy
Regarding Gaius's activities, John is elated to hear from "some brothers" (3 John 3), who were probably traveling missionaries and evangelists, that Gaius was still faithful to the truth and that his faith directed his actions. Gaius didn't just accept the truth as an intellectual proposition; he was "walking in the truth" (v. 4). He had not been swayed by false teachers; he had remained faithful to the gospel he had first received, possibly from John himself (v. 4).

One significant way in which Gaius lived out his faith was by offering hospitality. He received Christian travelers into his home so graciously that even though they were strangers when they arrived, they departed to tell others in the church about Gaius's love. With motels, hotels, and restaurants as common as they are today, it can be hard for us to understand how much travelers had to depend on hospitality in ancient times. When Jesus sent his disciples out to preach and teach, he told them, "Whatever town or village you enter, search for some worthy person there and stay at his house until you leave" (Matt. 10:11). Gaius was just such a worthy person.

An Open-Hand Policy
To John, hospitality was clearly more than merely a hot meal and a comfortable bed. It also included whatever support the traveler might need for the next part of the journey. "You will do well to send them on their way in a manner worthy of God," John urges Gaius. "It was for the sake of the Name that they went out, receiving no help from the pagans. We ought therefore to show hospitality to such men so that we may work together for the truth" (3 John 6-8).

Since some of the phrases may sound curious to us in these verses, let's reflect briefly on them here:

- "A manner worthy of God" sets a high standard for generosity, since God provides whatever we need, often before we are even aware of our needs.

- "Receiving no help from the pagans" is not a derogatory comment but rather a statement of fact about not having to depend on nonbelievers for support. John may well be alluding to an incident known to both he and Gaius in which a traveler was refused a bed and board by Christians and had to look among nonbelievers for a place to stay (see, for example, John's comments about Diotrophes in vv. 9-10). An incident like that would have been a great disappointment to John and to the rest of the church, since it was the responsibility of believers to show Christ's love by supporting the kingdom work carried out by traveling evangelists and teachers.

- "Working together for the truth" is a wonderful reminder that not everyone has to be on the road to take part in the missionary enterprise of the church. For example, my family and I recently chose to support the work of a missionary pilot in Indonesia. Even though only one person is flying the plane, all of this missionary's supporting families and churches play an important role in the work of proclaiming and living the truth.

Who's On First?
John next turns to the problem with Diotrephes, a leader of the church who has acted inhospitably, to say the least. John states that this leader "loves to be first," refuses to have anything to do with John (yet seems eager to gossip about him), refuses to offer hospitality to "the brothers," and even "stops those who want to do so and puts them out of the church" (vv. 9-10).

What could cause a leader to act in such a way? Jealousy? Greed? Fear of losing power or control? It's hardly a new story to hear of someone rising to a position of responsibility and becoming so enamored of his or her position that he or she is willing to abuse authority to keep it—and yet we always hope that church leaders will act differently. The good news is that we find very few people like Diotrephes singled out in the Bible, but the bad news is that we do find some. We always need to be on guard against people who want to be leaders simply for the sake of being in charge. "If anyone wants to be first, he must be the very last, and the servant of all" (Mark 9:35). Either Diotrephes was unfamiliar with this saying by Jesus, or he chose to ignore it.

Good Copies Require Good Originals
Not surprisingly, John tells Gaius not to copy the example of someone like Diotrephes. "Dear friend, do not imitate what is evil but what is good" (3 John 11). Imitating ungodly behavior is a constant temptation as believers watch people get ahead by lying, cheating, or stealing or simply by aggressive self-promotion. They seem to suffer no consequences, so the frustrated Christian may think, "Why not do likewise?"

LESSON 9: OPEN DOOR, OPEN HEART

This too is hardly a new story. An ancient psalmist laments, "O Lord, how long will the wicked be jubilant?" (Ps. 94:3). The longer we see the wicked enjoying the fruits of their behavior, the more foolish we feel in our feeble attempts to live by God's truth. But John commends us for our efforts: "Anyone who does what is good is from God. Anyone who does what is evil has not seen God" (3 John 11). John then cites a positive example shown by another believer: "Demetrius is well spoken of by everyone—and even by the truth itself. We also speak well of him, and you know that our testimony is true" (v. 12). The gospel itself testifies to the value of those who live by its truth; their lives are consistent with the good news taught and lived by Jesus.

Parting Thoughts

With a minor variation—"pen and ink" instead of "paper and ink"—John closes this letter with the same expression he used in his second letter. He hopes to visit Gaius soon, and he has much more to say in person.

John also sends a wish for peace and passes along the greetings of Gaius's friends in Christ. John's final request is that Gaius pass along greetings to their mutual friends by name. What a fitting ending for the only letter that John addresses to anyone by name!

Additional Notes

- vv. 1, 2, 5, 11—"Dear friend." As in John's first and second letters, the NIV continues to translate the Greek *agapeto* as "dear friend" instead of "beloved." Since John himself uses a different word for "friends" in verse 14 (*philos*), it would be preferable to convey the more accurate sense of "beloved" wherever the NIV has "dear friend."
- vv. 7-8—The *Didache,* an anonymous, second-century Christian writing purporting to convey the teaching of the twelve apostles, contains clear instructions about hospitality, including warnings about teachers who would take advantage of their listeners.
- v. 9—The letter to which John refers is an unknown letter. We might guess that "the church" John mentions is "the chosen lady" of 2 John 1, but there's no way to be sure. In 1 Corinthians 5:9-11 we find a reference to a similarly unknown letter by the apostle Paul (see also 2 Cor. 2:3-4).
- v. 12—John's statement "You know that our testimony is true" echoes a similar phrase near the end of his gospel account:

1, 2, 3 JOHN: LIVING IN THE LIGHT OF LOVE

"This is the disciple who testifies to these things and who wrote them down. We know that his testimony is true" (John 21:24). John is refreshingly unapologetic for speaking the plain truth.

GENERAL DISCUSSION

1. How would you describe the relationship between John and Gaius? On what was their relationship based? Is this kind of relationship rare or common in the church? What can individual Christians do to foster this kind of relationship?

2. What are some of the characteristics of good hospitality? How can hospitality be a witness for the gospel?

3. How do people like Diotrephes get into positions of leadership in the church? John says that Diotrephes "loves to be first" (3 John 9)—and yet what does Jesus say about being first? John also says that if he comes to visit Gaius, he will call attention to what Diotrephes has been doing. Could it be that others in the church are unaware of Diotrephes's actions, or perhaps of their danger to the church? Explain.

4. John says that Demetrius "is well spoken of by everyone—and even by the truth itself" (3 John 12). How does God's truth speak about any of us individually?

LESSON 9: OPEN DOOR, OPEN HEART

SMALL GROUP SESSION IDEAS

Opening (10-15 minutes)

Prayer—From the very earliest days of the Bible, hospitality has been one of the marks of God's people. Read Genesis 18:1-5; then use verse 3 as the opening of your prayer. Invite the Spirit of the Lord to join you as you study the Scriptures together, and to grant each of you wisdom and understanding for grace-filled living.

Share—If you have been reading books from the church library or from a Christian publisher's catalog (as suggested in Goalsetting, lesson 8), you may want to report briefly on what you've been reading. Has you reading been helpful in increasing your knowledge of the truth and strengthening your walk in obedience?

Or if you've decided as a group to choose another book to study, use this time to think and talk about what the next study will be.

Focus—John's third letter is the first one in which John mentions any individuals by name. Keep these questions in mind during your time of study: *Of the four people mentioned in this letter—John, Gaius, Diotrephes, or Demetrius—which one do I most resemble? Why? What would John say if he wrote a brief letter to me?*

Growing (30-35 minutes)

Read—Again (as suggested in the previous lesson) it may be helpful to read John's letter not only from the New International Version of the Bible but also from one or two other versions or paraphrases as well.

Discuss—Select several of the General Discussion questions to cover the content of John's letter; then choose from among the following questions to help further in bridging the gap from John's time to our own.

- What kind of greeting do you include when you write to friends? Acquaintances? Colleagues? Strangers? John addresses Gaius as "Dear friend" (or "Beloved"), adding the words, "whom I love in the truth" (3 John 1). Can you imagine using such a greeting? Why or why not?

- Do we pray about the spiritual needs and blessings of our friends and family as often as we pray about their physical concerns? Is one more important than the other? Explain.

- Recall a time when you were the recipient of exceptional hospitality. How did it make you feel? What effect did it have on your attitude?
- If you knew that Jesus was coming to your home, how would you prepare for his visit? Should we do any less for each other? Is this a fair question? Explain.
- What's the best way to deal with people like Diotrephes? (See 3 John 10.) How can we protect the church from their influence?
- John tells Gaius to imitate godly living; then he mentions Demetrius as a shining example (3 John 11-12). Whom would you like to imitate today? Why? What steps would you have to take to mirror that person's best qualities?

Goalsetting (5 minutes)
Think about some of the many possibilities for offering hospitality, and list them in order of how comfortable you would be with each one, for example:

- having one close friend over for coffee
- having a less well-acquainted couple over for dinner
- hosting a family of complete strangers (with half a dozen wild children) for the weekend.

When you've made a list, choose an option that's slightly beyond your comfort level and make a commitment to demonstrate that kind of hospitality soon.

Closing (10 minutes)
Preparing for Prayer—Since this is the final lesson of this study, take time to name some of the things or people for which you have been thankful during the course of this study. If this includes people within the group, tell them! As you also mention prayer requests, cite answered prayers as well.

Prayer—Return to the prologue of John's first letter. Read 1 John 1:1-4 together, and as you enter into prayer, thank God for the faithful way in which John fulfilled his calling as a servant, and for the miraculous way in which his letters have been preserved for us. Pray for each person who has been a part of the group, asking that each one may be better equipped and more willing to share the joy of his or her salvation.

To God be the glory!

Evaluation

Background

Size of group:
- ☐ fewer than 5 persons
- ☐ 5-10
- ☐ 10-15
- ☐ more than 15

Age of participants:
- ☐ 20-30
- ☐ 31-45
- ☐ 46-60
- ☐ 61-75 or above

Length of group sessions:
- ☐ under 60 minutes
- ☐ 60-75 minutes
- ☐ 75-90 minutes
- ☐ 90-120 minutes or more

Please check items that describe you:
- ☐ male
- ☐ female
- ☐ ordained or professional church staff person
- ☐ elder or deacon
- ☐ professional teacher
- ☐ church school or catechism teacher (three or more years' experience)
- ☐ trained small group leader

Study Guide and Group Process

Please check items that describe the material in the study guide:
- ☐ varied
- ☐ monotonous
- ☐ creative
- ☐ dull
- ☐ clear
- ☐ unclear
- ☐ interesting to participants
- ☐ uninteresting to participants
- ☐ too much
- ☐ too little
- ☐ helpful, stimulating
- ☐ not helpful or stimulating overly complex, long
- ☐ appropriate level of difficulty

Please check items that describe the group sessions:
- ☐ lively
- ☐ dull
- ☐ dominated by leader
- ☐ involved most participants
- ☐ relevant to lives of participants
- ☐ irrelevant to lives of participants
- ☐ worthwhile
- ☐ not worthwhile

In general I would rate this material as
- ☐ excellent
- ☐ very good
- ☐ good
- ☐ fair
- ☐ poor

Additional comments on any aspect of this Bible study:
- ☐ Name (optional):
- ☐ Church:
- ☐ City/State/Province:

Please send completed form to

Word Alive / 1, 2, 3 John
Faith Alive Christian Resources
2850 Kalamazoo Ave. SE
Grand Rapids, MI 49560

Thank you!